TALES OF SANTA BARBARA

TALES OF SANTA BARBARA

From Native Storytellers to Sue Grafton

Selected by

Steven Gilbar

&

Dean Stewart

John Daniel and Company
Santa Barbara, 1994
A Steven Gilbar Book

A Steven Gilbar Book
Published by John Daniel and Company
Post Office Box 21922
Santa Barbara, CA 93121

Book Design by Schlesinger Design

Library of Congress Cataloging-in-Publication Data
Tales of Santa Barbara : from native storytellers to Sue Grafton /
    Steven Gilbar.and Dean Stewart, editors.
            p.   cm.
        ISBN 1-880284-08-1
        1. American literature–California–Santa Barbara.
        2. Santa Barbara (Calif.)–Literary collections.
    I. Gilbar, Steven. II. Stewart, Dean.
    PS572.S35T35 1994
    810.8'0979491–dc20   94-18968
                                                               CIP

TABLE OF CONTENTS

DEAN STEWART

INTRODUCTION AND
A REMINISCENCE

THE CENTER OF DOWNTOWN SANTA BARBARA is the intersection of State and Anapamu Streets. I've heard that State is the most common name for a main street in cities and towns in America. Anapamu, on the other hand, I'm sure exists in only one town, Santa Barbara. It is a Chumash word meaning "the rising place." The crossroads' special charm, then, is that it is both typically American and uniquely local.

Small American towns are more alike than different. In Santa Barbara, as I've known it, there are echoes of Sherwood Anderson's *Winesburg, Ohio* and Thornton Wilder's *Our Town*. Even Faulkner's *The Hamlet*.

With some variations they tend to be static. The power relations, industry and agriculture, don't change much. Living in such a town, growing up in such a place, as I did in Santa Barbara, will have its characteristic range of experiences and limitations.

I've left and returned a few times, drawn back more by chance than special affection. When I first started traveling away from Santa Barbara in the early 1970s I discovered that many people had never heard of it, or knew of it only vaguely as a California beach town. Carmel, Del Mar, it was one of those little places. It's amusing to remember this now after a TV soap opera, an ex-President, and other publicizing events have made Santa Barbara immediately recognizable by name worldwide. But the place is actually known and not known. It has an image, a symbolic patina on the public mind.

It took me a long time to realize, to discover, that it has always been this way. At least in Santa Barbara's modern history. This was a town made famous by speculators, promoters and myth makers. The town of the picturesque old mission, hot springs and good weather. It was world famous before the turn of the century, declined and revived again in the 1920s, has disappeared and been rediscovered in small and large ways several times since. It is the past and the future of Santa Barbara.

Now obviously this is not a characteristic held in common by most small towns. But it is a frequent variation of the resort town, and there are scores of places, north and south, but most frequently in New England, that remind me of Santa Barbara in this way. These are towns not broadcasting but whispering their attractions as a getaway place, full-time if possible, or for a summer home or quiet vacation spot. Such places tend to carry with them images of splendor and wealth. In the case of Santa Barbara, it is part of the continuing glamour and public perception. The reality of such places is the exaggerated juxtaposition between rich and poor. This can be glaring and noticeable, but for reasons of lifestyle and proximity the environment is not particularly segregated. Snobbery has its enclaves but *noblesse oblige*, however condescending, is more the rule. Smugness and hypocrisy can be a prevailing tone, but for reasons of civic pride, a feeling of superiority is available to all. Servants imitate their employers, it has been said. And while I'm not trying to minimize anyone's hardship, I simply feel there are compensating factors. After all, everyone knows there are great bargains to be had shopping in thrift stores in a wealthy town.

The French writer Albert Camus had a similar conception of his youth in North Africa. In a few of his essays and travel pieces about Algiers and Oran for which I have a special fondness, he wrote of what the environment gave him despite the poverty of his circumstances. The quality of light and sunshine he considered a great blessing, a mysterious and ineffable nourishing source. To have grown up in a poor climate and without a beach to escape to would have been the really cruel injustice.

My situation was not so dire as Camus, but I know what he is trying to get at. Sometimes I ride my bicycle past the neighborhood where I grew up in the late 1950s and 60s, out along Modoc Road where I can get on the bike path to the University. My neighborhood was adjacent to Pilgrim Terrace, a collection of World War II barrack-style apartments that was public housing in Santa Barbara. It's a short bicycle ride, I often muse, from that place to the horse paddocks of Hope Ranch where the concentration of wealth is so great it makes much of Santa Barbara look like a village of paupers.

My old street is Kentia Place, a cul-de-sac butting up against a fence; beyond are the railroad tracks. Kentia is a type of palm but there is not one in sight. The street is planted with jacaranda. It is a street of boxed stucco apartments, very Southern California in type. The buildings are rundown now but the trees, battered by thirty years of children, have grown tall and strong. They bloom in lavender orbs and when the petals fall they circle the trunks in delicate pools.

In my boyhood, along the tracks and railroad right-of-way, there was a wilderness of an old lemon orchard and a few sycamores. It was a true hobo jungle for a time, with shanties and chicken coops. The city drove the squatters out finally with chain saws and fire. Later when the Mission Street underpass was dug early rains halted the work and created a lake. We played there, built a raft and pushed out onto the muddy water.

My family lived in a two-bedroom apartment. My grandmother had a room, my brother and I shared a room and my mother made her bed every night on the sofa. At my stuffy grade school in the middle class district of San Roque my friends were the sons and daughters of professionals. At home on Kentia, the men were carpenters and house painters. And there were some single mothers like mine who collected "aid to dependent children." Welfare, that is. And a social worker came around from time to time as well. To be of help? It seemed like they came to get counseling from my mother. They were young women, very good hearted, but full of romantic and marital and life-quandary problems. My mother befriended and advised them.

A firefighter lived over us for a few years and an undertaker lived next door for a long time. The undertaker was memorable because he dressed in a suit every day and on the few occasions I needed to wear a necktie he made the knot for me in a few quick gestures. By and by it occurred to me why he was so good at knotting a tie at other people's throats and ever since neckties have had a funereal aspect for me.

During the summer I took the bus across town to the Boy's Club where a Chicano man taught me to box, a Chinese man to swim, and a black man to play chess. I shot pool there and worked with the jigsaws in the shop. And if I tired of all that I could walk downtown, play pinball at the Greyhound Bus depot or go look for comic books or adventure stories at the Book Den or Public Library. I might end a long summer day having a Coke at the lunch counter of the old Woolworth's where The Earthling Bookstore is now located, across from the art museum at the corner of State and Anapamu.

Briefly, and in a very limited way, this has been my Santa Barbara: a universal and particular place. An American small town of class and race and neighborhood divisions, but in real and chimerical ways, more harmonious than discordant. An American archetype.

Over the years I've written a lot of local history. And the more I have done the more Santa Barbara feels like a Chinese box full of hidden parts, little compartments and surprises. Steven Gilbar and I have written a very complete literary history of Santa Barbara. It was a natural corollary of that project that well known and fugitive pieces of the written records of the place should be gathered together in an anthology. It is a box of delights, lyric, joyous and uncongenial. It informs us of the variety of ways the town has been experienced and can be known.

The original storytellers of Santa Barbara were the Chumash, an ancient people whose rich culture was nearly extinguished after contact with the Spanish explorers and missionaries. The mercurial and obsessive ethnographer John Peabody Harrington (1884-1961) began collecting their oral narratives in 1912. From his principal sources, Juan Justo (1859-1941), Maria Solares (18??-1922) and Fernando Librado (1804-1915) he gathered most of what is known today about the Chumash.

CHUMASH MYTHS

THE FLOOD. Maqutikok, Spotted Woodpecker, was the only one saved in the flood. He was Sun's nephew. Maria doesn't know why the flood came or how it started, but it kept raining and the water kept rising higher and higher until even the mountains were covered. All the people drowned except Maqutikok, who found refuge on top of a tree that was the tallest in the world. The water kept rising until it touched his feet, and the bird cried out, "Help me, Uncle, I am drowning, pity me!" Sun's two daughters heard him and told their father that his kinsman was calling for help. "He is stiff from cold and hunger," they said. Sun held his firebrand down low and the water began to subside. Maqutikok was warmed by the heat. Then Sun tossed him two acorns. They fell in the water near the tree and Maqutikok picked them up and swallowed them. Then Sun threw two more acorns down and the bird ate them and was content. That is why he likes acorns so much—they are still his food. And after the water was gone only Maqutikok remained. Maria has seen rocks in the mountains that are the exact shape of human arms and hands: they are the remains of the people who died in the flood. Those first people, the molmoloq_iku, were very tall. They used to wade across the channel without needing boats, taking chia and acorns and other things to the islanders in carrying nets. The very old men told Maria that people had found bones on Santa Rosa Island and at Mikiw which were human, but which were yards long.

THE MAKING OF MAN. After the flood Snilemun (the Coyote of the Sky), Sun, Moon, Morning Star, and Slo_w (the great eagle that knows what is to be) were discussing how they were going to make man, and Slo_w and Snilemun kept arguing about whether or not the new people should have hands like Snilemun. Coyote announced that there would be people in this world and they should all be in his image since he had the finest hands. Lizard was there also, but he just listened night after night and said nothing. At last Snilemun won the argument, and it was agreed that people were to have hands just like his. The next day they all gathered around a beautiful table-like rock that was there in the sky, a very fine white rock that was perfectly symmetrical and flat on top, and of such fine texture that whatever touched it left an exact impression. Snilemun was just about to stamp his hand down on the rock when Lizard, who had been standing silently just behind, quickly reached out and pressed a perfect hand-print into the rock himself. Snilemun was enraged and wanted to kill Lizard, but Lizard ran down into a deep crevice and so escaped. And Slo_w and Sun approved of Lizard's actions, so what could Snilemun do? They say that the mark is still impressed on that rock in the sky. If Lizard had not done what he did, we might have hands like a coyote today.

THE ORIGIN OF DEATH. Simplicio heard only that Coyote wanted to make people with hands like his but that Lizard wanted them to look like his hands instead, and Lizard won the argument. And later during the same conference Coyote proposed throwing man into a lake when he got old and making him young again. But the matavenado said no, the earth will get too full of people and there will be no room to stand. So Coyote lost out in this proposition also. The matavenado is

2

therefore also talked to and killed by the Ventureno, who tell it that it caused death.

ELEMENTS. The Indians adored three sacred "bodies"—earth, air and water. The sun was their chief god. They adored the sun. The sun was male and the moon was female. There were men among the old Indians to whom it was a pleasure to listen when they gave their views on this world. They were men of great ideas. They said that this earth was on top of the waters of the ocean, and that there were three elements concerning which we must be cautious—wind, rain, and fire. The rainbow is the shadow of these three elements that compose the world, and therefore it has three colors. The white is wind, the red is fire, and the blue is rain. The wind was sometimes called cenhes he_isup_, "breath of the world." And whenever there was lightning the old men would say, "Now beware, that is an element from the hand of the power that caused us to see this world." An old man told Fernando that thunder was the wind. All the winds get together up above. And sometimes there are whirlwinds so strong that they take the water and convert it into hail.

THE SUN. Fernando's grandfather told him that we say "the sun is made this way or that," but all we have are our ideas. He said that he and others before him had tried to figure out how the sun was made, but how could they? The sun is the beauty of the world—it is born in the east, giving the world beautiful light. They used to say that they had no idea as to who it was that created the sun. The morning and evening stars were the wives of the sun, for before sunrise the morning star comes first, then the dawn, and then the sun. The sun goes to rest in this hole (of the sand dollar) and leaves its rays outside while it rests inside. The sun was like a man. Whenever the dawn of morning comes be careful not to be misguided, for that is the breath of the sun who is a man. Fernando's grandfather used to tell him and other boys that when they heard a story they should listen carefully to the wording, which was metaphorical and enigmatic, so that they would get the substance of the story. Dawn is the sigh of the sun. The real name of the sun was kaqunup_mawa. This was its metaphorical name, and really meant "the radiance of the child born on the twenty-fourth of December."

THE SOUL. The old men when winnowing chia told Fernando that this world is merely a great flat winnowing tray. Some men move up and some down. And there is much chaff mixed through it all. The dead go west and are born again in this world. It is all a circle, an eddy within the abyss (_alampauwauhani). The Indians did absolutely nothing at the moment of death. They believed that the soul stayed around the old living place for five days after death, and that is why they fed it every night. But the soul of someone who was cremated went west with the flames and did not stay around for five days like the others. The soul of a drowned person always stayed in the sea, wandering, and never reached the land in the west or was born again. The soul of a baby that died before or after birth went west also, but it never reached the place that souls of adults did. They explained that the small surf fish never reached the place that the deep-water fish did. Fernando was told that the soul is eternal. The soul went to the west and at the end of twelve years it would return and live here reincarnated, born again. When Fernando was a boy and went out hunting the Indians used to tell him to be careful about shooting because the time was going to come—to be careful because there would be many young children. Those were pure spirits. They never slept. They were constantly on guard, watching and waiting for the spirits that were coming. Some spirits would go about the world, observing the nature of all others during those twelve years they inhabited another sphere, far in the west, very far from here. People would place food on the grave of a newly-buried person. They would celebrate for five days. They would cook meals early and at about four o'clock in the afternoon they would sit down to mourn and to scatter food. They scattered it with their hands, they scattered it to the four winds. Fernando's grandfather used to say that the "white people are a reincarnation of the souls that had gone west. They had a different color, were reincarnated in a lighter color, and spoke

4

a different language. The color and language of whites and Indians are different, but the noble principles of the soul are the same. For this world is a single congregation."

REINCARNATION. Silverio Qonoyo of Santa Inez, whose ancestors were all from Santa Rosa Island, once told Fernando the following story. The old men who understood such things once gathered together to discuss the nature of he who watches over us: Sun. Sun sees everything. "And those who die—how do they come to be born again?" asked one of that assembly. The wise man who was their leader answered, "They follow the sun. Every day they enter the portal of the sun. All over the world they die when the time comes for them to do so. He who dies will resurrect with the same feelings in his heart, but different in one respect—color." There was a sand dollar in that place that was lying mouth down, and the old man showed it to his companions and said, "Look at this—here in the middle" (between the tip of the middle petal of the flower and the rim). "The sun rises from the east and goes to the west, and all the spirits follow him. They leave their bodies. The sun reaches the door and enters, and the souls enter too. When it is time for the sun to fulfill his duty he emerges, for he lights the abysses with his eye, and all who are in the dusk resurrect."

THE SOUL'S JOURNEY TO SIMILAQSA. Three days after a person had been buried the soul comes up out of the grave in the evening. Between the third and fifth day it wanders about the world visiting the places it used to frequent in life. On the fifth day after death the soul returns to the grave to oversee the destruction of its property before leaving for Similaqsa. The soul goes first to Point Conception, which is a wild and stormy place. It was called humqaq. They only went near there to make sacrifices at a great sawil. There is place at humqaq below the cliff that can only be reached by rope, and there is a pool of water there like a basin, into which fresh water continually drips. And there in the stone can be seen the footprints of women and children.

There the spirit of the dead bathes and paints itself. Then it sees a light to the westward and goes toward it through the air, and thus reaches the land of Similaqsa.

Sometimes in the evening people at La Quemada village would see a soul passing by on its way to Point Conception. Sometimes these were the souls of people who had died, but sometimes they were souls that had temporarily left the body. The people of La Quemada would motion with their hands at the soul and tell it to return, to go back east, and they would clap their hands. Sometimes the soul would respond and turn back, but other times it would simply swerve a little from its course and continue on to Similaqsa. When the people of La Quemada saw the soul it shone like a light, and it left a blue trail behind it. The disease from which the person had died was seen as a fiery ball at its side. When the soul turned back, as it sometimes did, anyone at La Quemada who might have recognized it would hurry to the village where the man whose soul it was lived, and if the sick man then drank a lot of toloache he might recover and not die. Maria heard that a short time after the soul passed La Quemada the people there would hear a report like a distant cannon shot, and know that that was the sound of the closing of the gate at Similaqsa as the soul entered.

The old people said that there were three lands in the world to the west: wit, _ayaya, and Similaqsa. These were somewhat like purgatory, hell, and heaven. When the soul leaves Point Conception and crosses the sea, it first reaches the Land of Widows. When the women there get old their friends dip them in a spring and when they awake they are young again. And they never eat, though they have all kinds of food there. They merely take a handful of food and smell it and throw it away, and as soon as they do so it turns to feces. And when they are thirsty they just smell the water and their thirst is quenched. Once past the Land of Widows the soul comes to a deep ravine through which it must pass. The road is all cut up and consists of deep, fine earth as a result of so many souls passing over it. In the ravine are two huge stones that continually part and clash together, part and clash together, so that any person who got caught between them would be crushed. Any living person who attempted to pass would be killed, but souls pass through unharmed.

Once past the clashing rocks the soul comes to a place where there are two gigantic qaq perched on each side of the trail, and who each peck out an eye as the soul goes by. But there are many poppies growing there in the ravine and the soul quickly picks two of these and inserts them in each eye-socket and so is able to see again immediately. When the soul finally gets to Similaqsa it is given eyes made of blue abalone. After leaving the ravine the soul comes to La Tonadora, the woman who stings with her tail. She kills any living person who comes by, but merely annoys the soul who passes safely.

Once the soul has crossed the bridge it is safe in Similaqsa. There are two roads leading from the bridge—one goes straight ahead and the other goes to the left. Maria knows nothing about souls being born again in this world. Souls live in Similaqsa forever and never get old. It is packed full of souls. They harvest islay, sweet islay, and there is no end of it. Every kind of food is there in abundance. When children die they take the same route as adults. The qaq peck out their eyes, but they have no other troubles on the journey. They pass the bridge easily, for the monsters that try to frighten other souls do not appear.

A TOURIST,
AT THE OLD MISSION, SANTA BARBARA

He was a stranger in the land;
The Padre took him by the hand.
    He showed with pride the whitened towers,
    The bells that swing to mark the hours,
The skulls above the arched gate
With dust of years disconsolate,
    The Mission garden, planted when
    The Church was rich in serving men;
Then gravely asked, "And who are you
Who come our fallen state to view?"

The stranger straightened consciously:
"I am from Boston!" "Boston? Why,
    You speak the English language, friend,
    So well we all can comprehend
Your meaning! Yes, there have been men
From Boston here before you, when
    We could not understand a word
    Of all they said!" The tourist heard
And downward from the Mission went,
Contempt lost in astonishment.

In sandaled feet, with figure gowned
In coarse gray cloth, and rudely bound
    About the waist with ropes, I knew
    A marvel he must seem to you.
His life's as dusty as his gown;
Unknown beyond his native town.
    But more than yours is his surprise,
    To see the curious pride that lies
In one poor modern city's fame,
Which none of his old volumes name!

                 Camilla K. von K.
                     – 1887

Carobeth Laird (1895-1985) was married for a time to John Peabody Harrington while he was researching the Chumash. She recounted her adventures with this larger-than-life character in Encounter with an Angry God, *published in 1975.*

ENCOUNTER WITH AN ANGRY GOD

I DO REMEMBER ARRIVING at Santa Ynez in the spring of 1916, though I don't recall whether I got there by bus or horse-drawn stage. I have not forgotten the green beauty of the countryside or the thrill when Harrington met me and I knew that I was about to share his life and his career. I remember also my own foolish vanity and optimism. I carried the suitcase he had sent me and wore a navy blue skirt with a white shirtwaist, and navy blue straw hat with a red feather. I was resolved that, no matter what wilds we traveled in, I would always keep myself neat and attractive. So much for resolutions. The hat was soon lost, the blouse worn out, but the skirt lasted on; first spotted, then really soiled, then dirt-encrusted till it would all but stand alone. That dreadful blue serge skirt conditioned me, so that to this day if I am consulted about the color of a dress, I say, "Anything but navy blue." But at the time, at the beginning, having always had decent clothes I assumed that I always would.

Harrington's informant in Santa Ynez was a very ancient Chumash woman, Maria Solares. She must have been ninety or thereabouts. Her gentle face had the softness and fragility of something very old. Harrington took me to visit her and had me listen to her Chumash words, while he

smiled and cupped his ear and asked her to repeat until her patience wore
thin. Sometimes he would ask me about the way a word had sounded to
me, but I was not yet trusted to record anything on my own.

Maria spoke no English, and it pleased Harrington that I had enough
Spanish to make myself understood. She asked him, during an interview
at which I was not present, if I was *catolica*. Remembering that I had once
mentioned receiving infant baptism in the Methodist church, he told her
I was *metodista*, and that it was really the same thing. She enquired then if
they "ponen la cruz arriba" (put the cross above, presumably on top of
the churches), and being assured that they did, she relaxed and said I
would be a proper wife for him. I have no idea what Maria thought
Harrington's religion was; he scarcely knew enough ritual to deceive her.
Perhaps she thought religion was more important for a woman than a
man. Certainly she felt fondness and therefore a certain responsibility for
him; invariably courteous, she frequently treated him with the indulgence
that one would accord a child or a harmless madman.

I typed information which could be typed, and copied by hand
Chumash words containing sounds for which there were no symbols on
the Underwood. All this was put onto "slips," not cards but pieces of
paper cut to the size that Harrington had decided was most convenient
and printed with lines according to his specifications. (In matters con-
nected with his work, he was not averse to spending money, though he
always wanted to get good value.) Those slips were filed (at the time) in
cardboard boxes, a duplicate having been made for each Indian word and
miscellaneous item of information, so that they could be cross-filed. Ma-
terial piled up rapidly, and at one time got so far ahead of us that Harrington
hired a local high school girl, and I undertook to teach her our system of
filing. The experiment did not work out, but I remember that he spoke
admiringly of my patience and skill as a teacher. He really smiled at me
then, not a "hope to make a good impression" smile, but a genuine and
natural, warm and even loving smile, and I bloomed in its light.

Now I cannot, for the life of me, remember a single word of Maria's
native tongue, but other things that she said I shall never forget.

She had been told that before cattle were brought in to graze the land, the wild oats and other grasses had grown waist-high or even shoulder-high, and among the grass the lupine and other wildflowers all grew lush and tall, not stunted as we see them now. In those days the hunters did not have go afield, for deer and elk fed right outside the doors of the houses of the People. That had been in the good years. But once there came a great drought, the game went away, and there were no acorns, no seeds to gather, no roots to dig. This went on for several years. Many died. Women put hot water on their breasts to make milk to give their men strength, and all the fragments of buckskin, even the moccasins, were boiled and chewed. When finally all had resigned themselves to death, a runner came over the mountains from the village located near the site of what is now the town of Gaviota. He cried out that a whale was stranded on the beach. The people streamed through the rugged mountain passes and down to the sea carrying those who were too feeble to walk. There they feasted and grew strong. The decaying whale was big enough to nourish many people for a long time. When it was all gone, the rains came again, and the grasses and the game.

Maria also had stories and legends of mission and post-mission times. Her grandmother, she said, had been *esclava de la misión*. She had run away many, many times, and had been recaptured and whipped till her buttocks crawled with maggots. Yet she had survived to hand down her memories of the golden age before the white men came. Now her descendants were all very good Catholics.

A narrative of much more recent date concerned the dreadful fate that had almost befallen an Indian girl who was very beautiful and wild. She had an insatiable appetite for men, and it was implied that she might even have cast her eyes upon a young priest. Returning late one moonless night to her grandmother's home, she knew that something pursued her. She rushed into the house, slammed the door and pulled in the latch string. But there was still the cat hole, that little hole cut at the base of the door where the cat could go in and out at will. The long black arm of the Devil snaked through it and stretched clear across the room, extending a great hair clawed hand toward that unfortunate and undeserving girl. Had it not been that her grandmother was armed with something sacred—what I do not recall; it may have been a fragment of a palm branch left over from Palm Sunday or a blessed candle or even a little vial of holy water—she would surely have come to a most dreadful end. But threatened with the power of the Church, the monstrous arm of Satan shriveled and retreated.

These were the tales which lent their own peculiar patina to the places where I wandered. Actually, I cannot have had much time for wandering alone, but in retrospect these wanderings loom very large. The whole land was so exquisitely beautiful, so new to me and yet so mournfully touched with the light of its irretrievable past, Maria's lost Eden, in which fantasy and unwritten history were inextricably mingled. The roads were narrow and dusty, bordered by wild rose and elderberry bushes in full bloom. The stream was swift, clear, and shallow, winding sometimes through trees that met above it. In such a place, I saw a salmon, caught it with my hands, then put it back, not realizing that I had already completed its life cycle. At another time I watched a small, smooth, red, large-eyed creature walking slowly with primeval awkwardness over the smooth stones at the water's edge. I truly thought it was something not of this world, or at least hitherto unknown to men. Even after Harrington said it was a newt and not at all uncommon, the enchantment lingered.

Once, just once, during our first summer in Santa Ynez, Harrington took the whole day off from work. We walked away from the town, roaming over honey-colored hills dotted with great oak trees, their foliage so dark that it was almost black. Here and there grew clumps and thickets of lesser trees and shrubs, all strange to me because all of rural California was new and strange. Harrington knew their names, popular and scientific, but I remember only the buckeye with its creamy blossoms. It was an idyllic day. As we spoke of the Indians who had gathered acorns for centuries on these very hillsides, Harrington had an inspiration. He thought it would be beautiful and appropriate that we should take our clothes off and go about in a state of nature. The outcome was not happy. By nightfall I was suffering a high fever from sunburn.

12

Alfred Robinson (1806-1895) was part of the first generation of New England traders to descend upon the remote Spanish province of Alta California. One of the most important Americans in California before the Gold Rush, in his Life in California, published in 1846, he describes his first visit to Santa Barbara in 1829.

LIFE IN SANTA BARBARA

. . . C L O S E   U N D E R   O U R   L E E , we beheld the beautiful vale of Sta. Barbara.

Seen from the ship, the "Presidio" or town, its charming vicinity, and neat little Mission in the background, all situated on an inclined plane, rising gradually from the sea to a range of verdant hills, three miles from the beach, have a striking and beautiful effect. Distance, however, in this case, "lends enchantment to the view," which a nearer approach somewhat dispels; for we found the houses of the town, of which there were two hundred, in not very good condition. They are built in the Spanish mode, with *adobe* walls, and roofs of tile, and are scattered about outside the military department; shewing a total disregard of order on the part of the authorities. A ridge of rugged highlands extends along the rear, reaching from St. Buenaventura to Point Conception, and on the left of the town, in an elevated position, stands the *Castillo* or fortress.

The port of Santa Barbara is completely sheltered from the southwest and westerly winds, but somewhat exposed to those from the southeast. The anchorage is hard sand, abounding in seaweed, where the ship came to, in six and half fathoms. The sails were furled, the boat lowered and manned, and we proceeded to the shores.

* * *

At the landing we found our Yankee friend Daniel H——, and a few others who had come down to greet G——. As the town was three quarters of a mile distant, I accepted Daniel's offer of his fine saddled mule, and he getting up behind me, we rode along slowly, until we reached a small descent, where flowed a stream which recent rains had swollen beyond its usual bounds. Here the stubborn animal stopped, and seemed disinclined to proceed, but repeated application of the spurs at last urged him forward, and he forded the stream. Ascending the opposite bank, he again stopped, and giving a sudden fling in the air with his heels, sent us both rolling down towards the water. Fortunately we were neither wet nor hurt, but after so decided a manifestation of the creature's abilities, I declined remounting. Daniel, however, nowise disconcerted, mounted the beast and rode off alone.

As was requisite, we first visited the Commandant, in order to leave with him the ship's roll. This is a compliance exacted from all vessels arriving at ports in California, and usually their captains are obliged to deliver their documents in person.

The most stately house in the place at this time was that of the *diputado* to Mexico, Don José de la Guerra y Noriega. G—— having in his possession some presents for the family, we proceeded thither at once. Here we partook of chocolate with the lady of the house, Doña Maria Antonia, whilst her daughters eagerly distributed the several gifts. The old lady, a fine, motherly, good woman, had acquired by her deportment and affectionate manner toward strangers the esteem of all who knew her. Her father was an officer in the royal command, precious to the success of republicanism in Mexico, and her brothers, all but one, were then officers in the army. An American lady once observed to me, that there were in California two things supremely good, La Señora Noriega, and grapes!

During the afternoon, we visited the house of our friend Daniel. He was standing at the door anxiously awaiting our approach; and two or three children were playing in the corridor before him. As we drew near, the little ones retired, and chairs were brought outside, that we might enjoy the fresh air. Here we were to remain for the night, and arrangements were made accordingly. Supper was soon announced, when we had the pleasure of seeing the lady of the house, a fine healthy-looking female, with splendid eyes and beautiful black hair; but she said but little, and soon retired with her children.

The Presidio of Santa Barbara consists of a large square of buildings, surrounded by high walls, in plan similar to that of St. Diego, and contains a chapel, cemetery, prison, and storehouse. The Commandant, Don Romualdo Pacheco, is a Mexican, who came to the country in the year 1825, with the present Governor, Echeandia. The number of men garrisoned under his command does not exceed forty.

In the morning we walked to the Mission, distant from the town about half a league. The road was pleasant, through scattered oaks; and groups of cattle were seen grazing upon the grassy plains. On the right were spacious wheat fields; at length, through a narrow way, amid immense rocks scattered over the ground, we reached the establishment. The stone church, with its two towers and extensive wing, its artificial clock, tiled roofs, arched corridor, and majestic fountain, was before us. On the right were various buildings for superintendents, a guard-house, tannery, and a dilapidated grist-mill; on the left, the spacious garden, with its fruit trees and flowers, and several rows of low buildings. Father Antonio Jimeno, the missionary, received us in a small but tastefully arranged apartment; the floor of which was of colored cement, and the walls painted and hung round with pictures of saints. Two or three sofas, a long table and bookcase, comprised its furniture. He welcomed us kindly, and after a short conversation, we walked into the "patio," or square, where carpenters, saddlers, and shoemakers were at work, and young girls spinning and preparing wool for the loom. We next entered the vestry, which was carpeted and hung round with looking-glasses and fine paintings. Adjoining this was a small, but convenient dressing-room, where were arranged the numerous dresses and ornaments used in the church services, some of them rich and of the most costly description. From this, a door led into the church, where we beheld a gorgeous display of banners, paintings, images, and crucifixes of gold and silver. The musicians attached to the choir were practicing, and played some very fine airs; rather unsuitable, however, to the place. It was not unusual, both there and at the churches of other missions, to hear during the mass the most lively dancing tunes. Another door of the church opened upon the cemetery, where were buried the deceased Christians of the Mission and Presidio, surrounded by a thick wall, and having in one corner the charnel house, crowded with a ghastly array of skulls and bones.

In the rear, from a slight elevation, might be seen large fields of wheat and corn, and the little valleys among the hills, filled with fruit and vegetable gardens. A foaming stream rushes down the mountain, from which is carried in an open aqueduct along the brow of the hill, a supply of water for a spacious reservoir of beautiful masonry.

We returned to town, and at the beach found a lively and busy scene. Our men were passing through the surf to the launch bearing hides upon their heads, while others landed, from smaller boats, portions of the ship's cargo. It was a merry sight, and the shouts mingled with the sound of the waves as they beat upon the sand. We embarked on board ship, where soon our decks were crowded with men and women of all classes; many coming to purchase, some to see the vessel, and others to accompany their friends, so that it was not unusual for us to have a party of twenty or thirty at dinner.

The dress worn by the middling class of female is a chemise with short embroidered sleeves, richly trimmed with lace, a muslin petticoat flounced with scarlet, and secured at the waist by a silk band of the same color, shoes of velvet or blue satin, a cotton *reboso* or scarf, pearl necklace and ear-rings, with the hair falling in broad plaits down the back. Others of the higher class dress in the English style, and instead of the *reboso* substitute a rich and costly shawl of silk or satin. There is something graceful in the management of the *reboso* that the natives alone can impart, and the perfect nonchalance with which it is thrown about them and worn, adds greatly to its beauty.

Very few of the men have adopted our mode of dress, the greater part adhering to the ancient costume of the past century. Short clothes, and

16

jacket trimmed with scarlet, a silk sash about the waist, *botas* of ornamental and embroidered deer skin, secured by colored garters, embroidered shoes, the hair long, braided and fastened behind with ribbons, a black silk handkerchief around the head, surmounted by an oval and broad-brimmed hat, is the dress universally worn by the men of California.

* * *

About this time we were much alarmed, in consequence of the burning of the woods upon the mountains. For several days the smoke had been seen to rise from the distant hills of St. Buenaventura, and gradually approached the town. At last it had reached the confines of the settlement, and endangered the fields of grain, and gardens. Soon it spread low upon the hills, and notwithstanding a strong westerly wind was blowing, the flames travelled swiftly to windward, consuming everything in their course. It was late at night when they reached the rear of the town, and as they furiously wreathed upwards, the sight was magnificent, but terrible. The wind blew directly upon the town, and the large cinders that fell in every direction seemed to threaten us with certain destruction. The air was too hot to breathe. The inhabitants fled from their homes to the beach, or sought the house of Señor Noriega, where prayers were offered and the saints supplicated. The vessels at anchor in the bay were also much endangered, for their decks were literally covered with burning cinders, and their crews incessantly employed in keeping them wet. During the entire night the ravages of the fire continued, and when daylight broke it had seized upon the vineyard belonging to the Mission. Here the green state of vegetation somewhat checked its progress, and it passed over to the mountains again, to pursue its course northward. On the uplands everything was destroyed, and, for months afterwards, the bare and blackened hills marked the course of the devastating element.

* * *

17

As we rode along we had an excellent opportunity of seeing the different varieties of riding, common in the country. The universal mode of traveling, with both males and females, is on horseback; the latter generally ride with a person behind them, who guides the horse. In this way many were returning from the Mission. Now and then we passed a poor broken-down horse with three lazy vagabonds astride him, who unfeelingly beat and spurred him onward. A few old men came trotting along, who from their firm manner of riding with their legs clinging to the sides of their horses, seemed almost to have grown to them. More amusing still, we saw many children of not more than three of four years of age, two or three together on one horse, who appeared as secure in their seats as the old men who had lived a lot of their lives in the saddle. The young commence thus early their lessons in horsemanship, and when dispatched by their parents on some errand, the two more expert riders seat the youngest between them, and go tearing across the country without the least apprehension, not infrequently with a bullock's hide dragging over the ground behind them. Both young and old are passionately fond of riding, and rarely go from one house to another, no matter how short the distance, except on horseback. Many take their meals in the saddle, and the poor animal is fortunate if he gets either food or drink till late at night, when his master quits his back for his bed and retires to repose.

I sat down at my door on my return, to enjoy the following lively scene. In the front of the house was a large square, where the Indians assembled on Sunday afternoons, to indulge in their favorite sports and purse their chief amusement—gambling. Here members were gathered together in little knots, who appeared engaged in angry conversation; they were adjusting, as Daniel informed me, the boundary lines for the two parties who were to play that afternoon at ball, and were thus occupied till dinner time. When I returned from dinner they had already commenced, and at least two or three hundred indians of both sexes were engaged in the game. It was the "Presidio" against the "Mission." They played with a small ball of hard wood, which, when hit, would bound with tremendous force without striking the ground for two or three hundred yards. Great excitement prevailed, and immense exertion was manifested on both sides, so that it was not till late in the afternoon that the game was decided in favor of the Indians of the Presidio.

Many of the Indians retired afterwards to the enjoyment of their *Temescal* or hot air baths, which is their usual resort after fatigue, and is the sovereign remedy for nearly all their diseases. A round hovel or oven of mud is built, generally, over an excavation in the ground. An opening is left in the roof for the escape of the smoke, and one at the side, for entrance. As many persons as it can conveniently hold, enter, and make a fire close to the door on the inside. They continue to add fuel to the flame till they can no longer bear the intense heat, which throws them into a profuse perspiration. Thoroughly exhausted, they crawl forth from the hut, and plunge themselves headlong into the nearest stream. I have frequently seen the old men lying about on the floor of the oven apparently bereft of all their strength, whilst some of the younger persons enjoyed it, and sang and laughed under its influence. The women also frequently make use of these baths, repeating them till their diseases are cured.

* * *

A few leagues from Santa Barbara is a hot spring, where the inhabitants resort in some cases of disease. I accompanied a few friends to the place, one of whom was desirous of proving the efficacy in curing rheumatism. We rode across the little settlement of Montecito, and soon came to a rough and a narrow passage leading to the mountains, which we ascended till the path became so intricate that it was impossible to proceed further on horseback, so dismounting and securing our horses, we walked to the spring, where the waters were boiling up with much force. The place was very rocky, and the stream had washed away the earth, forming numerous cavities sufficiently large to contain one person. These were filled with water of different temperatures, varying according to the distance from the source of the spring, where in some places was so hot that I could not bear my hand in it. There are a few shanties on the spot for the accommodation of families, who frequently pass several days there sharing the summer months. After bathing, we returned home to the town, much enervated from the peculiar character of the waters.

FULL MOON
(Santa Barbara)

I listened, there was not a sound to hear
    In the great rain of moonlight pouring down,
The eucalyptus trees were carved in silver,
    And a light mist of silver lulled the town.

I saw far off the grey Pacific bearing
    A broad white disk of flame,
And on the garden-walk a snail beside me
    Tracing in crystal the slow way he came.

Sara Teasdale
— *1920*

Richard Henry Dana, Jr. (1815-1878) dropped out of Harvard at nineteen to sign on as a common seamen on a merchant ship headed to California to purchase hides. His memoir of that experience, Two Years Before the Mast *(1840), contains a description of Alfred Robinson's wedding.*

A FANDANGO

GREAT PREPARATIONS WERE MAKING on shore for the marriage of our agent [Alfred Robinson] and Doña Anita de la Guerra de Noriega y Carrillo, youngest daughter of Don Antonio Noriega, the grandee of the place, and the head of the first family in California. Our steward was ashore three days, making pastry and cake, and some of the best of our stores were sent off with him. On the day appointed for the wedding, we took the captain ashore in the gig, and had orders to come for him at night, with leave to go up to the house and see the fandango. Returning on board, we found preparations making for a salute. Our guns were loaded and run out, men appointed to each, cartridges served out, matches lighted, and all the flags ready to be run up. I took my place at the starboard after-gun, and we all waited for the signal from on shore. At ten o'clock the bride went up with her sister to the confessional, dressed in deep black. Nearly an hour intervened, when the great doors of the mission church opened, the bells rang out a loud discordant peal, the private signal for us was run up by the captain ashore, the bride, dressed in complete white, came out of the church with the bridegroom, followed by a long procession. Just as she stepped from the church door, a small white cloud issued from the bows of our ship, which was full in sight, the loud report echoed among the surrounding hills and over the bay, and instantly the ship was dressed in flags and pennants from stem to stern. Twenty-three guns followed in regular succession, with an interval of fifteen seconds between each, when the cloud blew off, and our ship lay dressed in her colors all day. At sundown another salute of the same number of guns was fired, and all the flags run up. This we thought was pretty well—a gun every fifteen seconds—for a merchantman with only four guns and a dozen or twenty men.

After supper the gig's crew were called, and we rowed ashore, dressed in our uniform, beached the boat, and went up to the fandango. The bride's father's house was the principal one in the place, with a large court in front, upon which a tent was built, capable of containing several hundred people. As we drew near, we heard the accustomed sound of violins and guitars, saw a great motion of the people within. Going in, we found nearly all the people of the town—men, women, and children—collected and crowded together, leaving barely room for the dancers; for on these occasions no invitations are given, but everyone is expected to come, though there is always of private entertainment within the house for particular friends. The old women sat down in rows, clapping their hands to the music, and applauding the young ones. The music was lively, and among the tunes, we recognized several of our popular airs, which we, without doubt, have taken from the Spanish. In the dancing I was much disappointed. The women stood upright, with their hands down by their sides, their eyes fixed upon the ground before them, and slid about without any perceptible means of motion; for their feet were invisible, the hem of their dresses forming a circle about them, reaching to the ground. They looked as grave as though they were going through some religious ceremony, their faces as little excited as their limbs; and on the whole, instead of the spirited, fascinating Spanish dances which I had expected, I found the Californian fandango, on the part of the women at least, a lifeless affair. The men did better. They danced with grace and spirit, moving in circles round their nearly stationary partners, and showing their figures to advantage.

A great deal was said about our friend Don Juan Bandini, and when he did appear, which was towards the close of the evening, he certainly gave us the most graceful dancing that I had ever seen. He was dressed in white pantaloons, neatly made, a short jacket of dark silk, gaily figured, white stockings, and thin morocco slippers upon his very small feet. His slight and graceful figure was well adapted to dancing, and he moved about with the grace and daintiness of a young fawn. An occasional touch of the toe to the ground seemed all that was necessary to give him a long interval of motion in the air. At the same time he was not fantastic or flourishing, but appeared to be rather repressing a strong tendency to motion. He was loudly applauded, and danced frequently towards the close of the evening. After the supper the waltzing began, which was confined to a very few of the *gente de razón*, and was considered a high accomplishment, and a mark of aristocracy. Here, too, Don Juan figured greatly, waltzing with the sister of the bride (Doña Angustia, a handsome woman and a general favorite) in a variety of beautiful figures, which lasted as much as half an hour, no one else taking the floor. They were repeatedly and loudly applauded, the old men and women jumping out of their seats in admiration, and the young people waving their hats and handkerchiefs. The great amusement of the evening—owing to its being the Carnival— was the breaking of eggs filled with cologne or other essences, upon the heads of the company. The women bring a great number of these secretly about them, and the amusement is to break one upon the head of a gentleman when his back is turned. He is bound in gallantry to find out the lady, and return the compliment, though it must not be done if the person sees you. A tall, stately Don, with immense gray whiskers, and a look of great importance, was standing before me, when I felt a light hand on my shoulder, and, turning around, saw Doña Angustia (whom we all knew, as she had been up to Monterey and down again, in the *Alert*), with her finger upon her lip motioning me gently aside. I stepped back a little, when she went up behind the Don, and with one hand knocked off his huge *sombrero*, and at the same instant, with the other, broke the egg upon his head, and, springing behind me, was out of sight in a moment. The Don turned slowly round, the cologne running down his face and over his clothes, and a loud laugh breaking out from every quarter. He looked

23

around in vain for some time, until the direction of so many laughing eyes showed him the fair offender. She was his niece, and a great favorite with him, so old Don Domingo had to join in the laugh. A great many such tricks were played, and many a war of sharp maneuvering was carried on between couples of the younger people, and at every successful exploit a general laugh was raised.

Another of their games I was for some time at a loss about. A pretty young girl was dancing, named—after what would appear to us an almost sacrilegious custom of the country—Espíritu Santu, when a young man went behind her and placed his hat directly upon her head, letting it fall down over her eyes, and sprang back among the crowd. She danced for some time with the hat on, when she threw it off, which called forth a general shout, and the young man was obliged to go out upon the floor and pick it up. Some of the ladies, upon whose heads hats had been placed, threw them off at once, and a few kept them on throughout the dance, and took them off at the end, and held them out in their hands, when the owner stepped out, bowed, and took it from them. I soon began to suspect the meaning of the thing, and was afterwards told that it was a compliment, and an offer to become a lady's gallant for the rest of the evening, and to wait upon her home. If the hat was thrown off the offer was refused, and the gentleman was obliged to pick up his hat amid a general laugh. Much amusement was caused sometimes by gentlemen putting hats on the ladies' heads without permitting them to see whom it was done by. This obliged them to throw them off, or keep them on at a venture, and when they came to discover the owner the laugh was turned upon one or the other.

The captain sent for us about ten o'clock, and we went aboard in high spirits, having enjoyed the new scene much, and were of great importance among the crew, from having so much to tell, and from the prospect of going every night until it was over; for these fandangos generally last three days. The next day two of us were sent up to the town, and took care to come back by way of Señor Noriega's, and take a look into the booth. The musicians were again there, upon their platform, scraping and twanging away, and a few people, apparently of the lower classes, were dancing. The dancing is kept up at intervals throughout the day, but the crowd, the spirit, and the *elite* come in at night. The next night, which was the last, we went ashore in the same manner, until we got almost tired of the monotonous twang of the instruments, the drawling sounds which the women kept up, as an accompaniment, and the slapping of the hands in time with the music, in place of castanets. We found ourselves as great objects of attention as any persons or anything at the place. Our sailor dresses—and we took great pains to have them neat and ship-shape—were much admired, and we were invited, from every quarter, to give them an American dance; but after the ridiculous figure some of our countrymen cut in dancing after the Mexicans, we thought it best to leave it to their imaginations. Our agent, with a tight black swallow-tailed coat just imported from Boston, a high stiff cravat, looking as if he had been pinned and skewered, with only his feet and hands left free, took the floor just after Bandini, and we thought they had had enough of Yankee grace.

The last night they kept it up in great style, and were getting into a high go, when the captain called us off to go aboard, for, it being southeaster season, he was afraid to remain on shore long; and it was well he did not, for that night we slipped our cables, as a crowner to our fun ashore, and stood off before a south-easter, which lasted twelve hours, and returned to our anchorage the next day.

THE GARDEN
(Mission Hill, Santa Barbara)

My garden lies in the heart of the world
    Begirt by mountain heights,
Blue, and silver, and crimson impearled
    In the lovely eventing lights,
And beyond it stretches the azure sea;
O the depth, and mystery!

In the heart of my garden I can hear
    The heart of the world as it beats,
For from the tower standing near
    Time day by day repeats
Prime and matins, and noon and nones.
The bells chant the hours in solemn tones.

My garden's heart has the olive trees' shade,
    And the date palms whisper low;
Tacomas have an arbor made,
    Acacias shed golden snow;
For here the climates all combine
With palms and cypress, orange and pine.

And in the heart of my garden repose
    All flowers beneath the sun,—
Myrtle and aloes, and aster and rose
    And lavender, every one;
For it takes tribute from every land;
Lotus and lilac together stand.

My garden's heart has an eye of the soul,
    For near the deodar
Lies a placid pool which mirrors the whole
    Of all the things that are.
Sun, moon, and stars, and flower and tree,
And time and space, and you, and me.

The inmost heart of the heart of the world
    Here in my garden lies,
For life is in every blossom curled,
    In every wing that flies.
'Tis a home of love, of care's surcease,
And all its paths are paths of peace.

Caroline Hazard
— 1927

Edwin Bryant (1805-1869) volunteered to join John C. Fremont's battalion to assist Commodore Stockton in suppressing a rebellion of Californios against the American takeover. His notes describe the battalion's epic passage of San Marcos Pass in 1846.

WHAT I SAW IN SANTA BARBARA

DECEMBER 22.—Clear and pleasant. Being of the party which performed rear-guard duty today, with orders to bring in all stragglers, we did not leave camp until several hours after the main body had left. The horses of the *caballada* and the pack-animals were continually giving out and refusing to proceed. Parties of men, exhausted, lay down upon the ground, and it was with much urging, and sometimes with peremptory commands only, that they could be prevailed upon to proceed. The country bears the same marks of drought heretofore described, but fresh vegetation is now springing up and appears vigorous. A large horse-trail leading into one the *cañadas* of the mountains on our left, was discovered by the scouts, and a party was dispatched to trace it. We passed one deserted *rancho*, and reached camp between nine and ten o'clock at night, having forced in all the men and most of the horses and pack-mules. Distance 15 miles.

December 23.—Rain fell steadily and heavily the entire day. A small party of men was in advance. Discovering in a brushy valley two Indians armed with bows and arrows, they were taken prisoners. Learning from them that there was a *caballada* of horses secreted in one of the *cañadas*, they continued on about ten miles, and found about twenty-five fresh, fat horses, belonging to a Californian now among the insurgents below.

They were taken and delivered at the camp near the eastern base of the St. Ynes mountains. Passed this morning a *rancho* inhabited by a foreigner, an Englishman.

December 24.—Cloudy and cool, with an occasional sprinkling rain. Our route today lay directly over the St. Ynes mountains, by an elevated and most difficult pass. The height of this mountain is several thousand feet. We reached the summit about twelve o'clock, and our company composing the advance-guard, we encamped about a mile and a half in advance of the main body of the battalion, at a point which overlooks the beautiful plain of Santa Barbara, of which, and the ocean beyond, we had a most extended and interesting view. With the spyglass we could see, in the plain far below us, herds of cattle quietly grazing upon the green herbage that carpets its gentle undulations. The plain is dotted with groves, surrounding the springs and belting the small watercourses, of which there are many flowing from this range of mountains. *Ranchos* are scattered far up and down the plain, but not one human being could be seen stirring. About ten or twelve miles to the south, the white towers of the mission of Santa Barbara raise themselves. Beyond, is the illimitable waste of waters. A more lovely and picturesque landscape I never beheld. On the summit of the mountain, and surrounding us, there is a growth of hawthorn, manzanita, (in bloom), and other small shrubbery. The rock is soft sandstone and conglomerate, immense masses of which, piled one upon another, for a wall along the western brow of the mountain, through which there is a single pass or gateway about eight or ten feet in width. The descent on the western side is precipitous, and appears almost impassable. Distance 4 miles.

December 25.—Christmas day, and a memorable one to me. Owing to the difficulty in hauling the cannon up the steep acclivities of the mountain, the main body of the battalion did not come up with us until twelve o'clock, and before we commenced the descent of the mountain a furious storm commenced, raging with a violence rarely surpassed. The rain fell in torrents and the wind blew almost with the force of a tornado. This fierce strife of the elements continued without abatement the entire afternoon, and until two o'clock at night. Driving our horses before us we were compelled to slide down the steep and slippery rocks, or wade through deep gullies and ravines filled with mud and foaming torrents of water, that rushed downwards with such force as to carry along the loose rocks and tear up the trees and shrubbery by the roots. Many of the horses falling into the ravines refused to make an effort to extricate themselves, and were swept downwards and drowned. Others, bewildered by the fierceness and terrors of the storm, rushed or fell headlong over the steep precipices and were killed. Others obstinately refused to proceed, but stood quaking with fear or shivering with cold, and many of these perished in the night from the severity of the storm. The advance party did not reach the foot of the mountain and find a place to encamp until night—and a night of more impenetrable and terrific darkness I never witnessed. The ground upon which our camp was made, although sloping from the hills to a small stream, was so saturated with water that men as well as horses sunk deep at every step. The rain fell in such quantities that fires with great difficulty could be lighted, and most of them were immediately extinguished.

The officers and men belonging to the company having the cannon in charge, labored until nine or ten o'clock to bring them down the mountain, but they were finally compelled to leave them. Much of the baggage also remained on the side of the mountain, with the pack-mules and horses conveying them; all efforts to force the animals down being fruitless. The men continue to straggle into the camp until a late hour of the night; some crept under the shelving rocks and did not come in until the next morning. We were so fortunate as to find our tent, and after much difficulty pitched it under an oak-tree. All efforts to light a fire and keep it blazing proving abortive, we spread our blankets upon the ground and endeavored to sleep, although we could feel the cold streams of water running through the tent and between and around our bodies.

In this condition we remained until about two o'clock in the morning, when the storm having abated, I rose, and shaking from my garments the dripping water, after many unsuccessful efforts succeeded in kindling a fire. Near our tent I found three soldiers who had reached camp at a late hour. They were fast asleep on the ground, the water around them being two or three inches deep; but they had taken care to keep their heads above water by using a log of wood for a pillow. The fire beginning to blaze freely, I dug a ditch with my hands and a sharp stick of wood, which drained off the pool surrounding the tent. One of the men, when he felt the sensation consequent upon being "high and dry," roused himself, and sitting upright, looked around for some time with an expression of bewildered amazement. At length he seemed to realize the true state of the case, and exclaimed in a tone of energetic soliloquy:

"Well, who wouldn't be a soldier and fight for California?"

"You are mistaken," I replied.

Rubbing his eyes he gazed at me with astonishment, as if having been entirely unconscious of my presence; but reassuring himself he said:

"How mistaken?"

"Why," I answered, "you are not fighting for California."

"What the d—then am I fighting for?" he inquired.

"For TEXAS."

"Texas be d—d; but hurrah for General Jackson!" and with this exclamation he threw himself back again upon his wooden pillow, and was soon snoring in a profound slumber.

Making a platform composed of sticks of wood upon the soft mud, I stripped myself to the skin, wringing the water from each garment as I proceeded. I then commenced drying them by the fire in the order that they were replaced upon my body, an employment that occupied me until daylight, which sign, above the high mountain to the east, down which we had rolled rather than marched yesterday, I was truly rejoiced to see. Distance 3 miles.

December 26.—Parties were detailed early this morning, and dispatched up the mountain to bring down the cannon, and collect the living horses and baggage. The destruction of horse-flesh, by those who witnessed the scene, by daylight, is described as frightful. In some places large numbers of dead horses were piled together. In others, horses half buried in the mud of the ravines, or among the rocks, were gasping in the agonies of death. The number of dead animals is variously estimated at from seventy-five to one hundred and fifty, by different persons. The cannon, most of the missing baggage, and the living horses, were all brought in by noon. The day was busily employed in cleansing our rifles and pistols, and drying our drenched baggage.

December 27.—Preparations were commenced early for the resumption of our march; but such was the condition of everything around us, that it was two o'clock, P.M., before the battalion was in readiness; and then so great had been the loss of horses in various ways, that the number remaining was insufficient to mount the men. One or two companies, and portions of others, were compelled to march on foot. We were visited during the forenoon by Mr. Sparks, an American, Dr. Den, an Irishman, and Mr. Barton, another American, residents of Santa Barbara. They had been suffered by the Californians to remain in the place. Their information communicated to us was that the town was deserted of nearly all its population. A few houses only were occupied. Passing down a beautiful and fertile undulating plain, we encamped just before sunset in a live-oak grove, about half a mile from the town of Santa Barbara. Strict orders were issued by Col. Fremont, that the property and the persons of Californians, not found in arms, should be sacredly respected. To prevent all collisions, no soldier was allowed to pass the lines of the camp without special permission, or orders from his officers.

I visited the town before dark; but found the houses, with few exceptions, closed, and the streets deserted. After hunting about some time we discovered a miserable dwelling, occupied by a shoemaker and his family, open. Entering it we were very kindly received by its occupants, who, with a princely supply of civility, possessed but a beggarly array of comforts. At our request they provided for us a supper of *tortillas, frijoles,* and stewed *carne,* seasoned with *chile colorado* for which, paying them *dos pesos* for four, we bade them good-evening, all parties being well satisfied. The family consisted, exclusive of the shoemaker, of a dozen women and children, of all ages. The women, from the accounts they had received of the intentions of the Americans, were evidently unprepared for civil treatment from them. They expected to be dealt with in a very barbarous manner, in all respects; but they were disappointed, and invited us to visit them again. Distance 8 miles.

The battalion remained encamped at Santa Barbara, from the 27th of December to the 3d of January, 1847. The U.S. flag was raised in the public square of the town the day after our arrival.

The town of Santa Barbara is beautifully situated for the picturesque, about one mile from the shore of a roadstead, which affords anchorage for vessels of any size, and a landing for boats, in calm weather. During stormy weather, or the prevalence of strong winds from the southeast, vessels, for safety, are compelled to stand out to sea. A fertile plain extends some twenty or thirty miles up and down the coast, varying in breadth from two to ten miles, and bounded on the east by a range of high mountains. The population of the town, I should judge from the number of houses, to be about 1200 souls. Most of the houses are constructed of adobes, in the usual architectural style of Mexican buildings. Some of them, however, are more Americanized, and have some pretensions to tasteful architecture, and comfortable and convenient interior arrangement. Its commerce, I presume, is limited to the export of hides and tallow produced upon the surrounding plain; and the commodities received in exchange for these from the traders on the coast. Doubtless, new and yet undeveloped sources of wealth will be discovered hereafter, that will render this town of much greater importance than it is at present.

On the coast, a few miles above Santa Barbara, there are, I have been told, immense quantities of pure bitumen or mineral tar, which, rising in the ocean, has been thrown upon the shore by the waves, where in a concrete state, like rosin, it has accumulated in inexhaustible masses. There are, doubtless, many valuable minerals in the neighboring mountains, which, when developed by enterprise, will add greatly to the wealth and importance of the town. For intelligence, refinement, and civilization, the population, it is said, will compare advantageously with any in California. Some old and influential Spanish families are residents of this place; but their casas, with the exception of that of Señor Don José Noriega, the largest house in the place, are now closed and deserted. Senor N. is one of the oldest and most respectable citizens of California, having filled the highest offices in the government of the country. One of his daughters is a resident of New York, having married Alfred Robinson, Esq., of that city, author of *Life in California.*

The climate, judging from the indications while we remained here, must be delightful, even in winter. With the exception of one day which was tempestuous, the temperature at night did not fall below 50, and during the day the average was between 60 and 70. The atmosphere was perfectly clear and serene, the weather resembling that of the pleasant days of April in the same latitude on the Atlantic side of the continent. It is a peculiarity of the Mexicans that they allow no shade or ornamental trees to grow near their houses. In none of the streets of the towns or missions through which I have passed, has there been a solitary tree standing. I noticed very few horticultural attempts in Santa Barbara. At the mission, about two miles distant, which is an extensive establishment and in good preservation, I was told that there were fine gardens, producing most of the varieties of fruits of the tropical and temperate climates.

Several Californians came into camp and offered to deliver themselves up. They were permitted to go at large. They represented that the Californian force in the south was daily growing weaker from dissensions and desertions. The United States prize-schooner Julia, arrived on the 30th, from which was landed a cannon for the use of the battalion. It has, however, to be mounted on wheels, and the gear necessary for hauling it has to be made in the camp. Reports were current in camp on the 31st, that the Californians intended to meet and fight us at San Buenaventura, about thirty miles distant. On the 1st of January, the Indians of the mission and town celebrated New-Year's day, by a procession, music, etc. They marched from the mission to the town, and through most of the empty and otherwise silent streets. Among the airs they played was "Yankee Doodle."

33

January 3.—A beautiful spring-like day. We resumed our march at 11 o'clock, and encamped in a live-oak grove about ten miles south of Santa Barbara. Our route has been generally near the shore of the ocean. Timber is abundant, and the grass and other vegetation luxuriant. Distance 10 miles.

January 4.—At the "Rincon," or passage between two points of land jutting into the ocean, so narrow that at high tides the surf dashes against the nearly perpendicular bases of the mountains which bound the shore, it has been supposed the hostile Californians would make a stand, the position being so advantageous to them. The road, if road it can be called, where all marks of hoofs or wheels are erased by each succeeding tide, runs along a hard sand-beach, with occasional projections of small points of level ground, ten or fifteen miles, and the surf, even when the tide has fallen considerably, frequently reaches to the bellies of the horses. Some demonstration has been confidently expected here, but we encamped in this pass the first day without meeting an enemy or seeing a sign of one. Our camp is close to the ocean, and the roar of the surf, as it dashes against the shore, is like that of an immense cataract. Hundreds of the grampus whale are sporting a mile or two distance from the land, spouting up water, and spray to a great height, in columns resembling steam from the escape-pipes of steamboats. Distance 6 miles.

GERTRUDE ATHERTON

Gertrude Atherton (1857-1948), the famous San Francisco novelist, traveled down to Santa Barbara with her sister Aleece in 1892. It was her intention to soak up atmosphere and meet the De la Guerra family for a planned novel, The Doomswoman. *Her mission was a success and was recounted years later in her autobiography.*

ADVENTURES IN SANTA BARBARA

FROM SAN LUIS OBISPO we went to Santa Ynez, an isolated Mission surrounded by silver olive groves, no doubt planted by the old padres. The priest gave us a luncheon of macaroni, and detained us as long as possible, for he was a lonely soul. He showed us some illuminated manuscripts made in the old days by his predecessors when not engaged in the hopeless task of spiritualizing the lowest race of Indians on the continent.

Thence we took the stage for Santa Barbara. We could have gone far more comfortably by train from San Luis, but I wanted to describe from personal observation De la Vega's ride over the mountains on his ill-fated quest. And this time I was well rewarded, for the scenery was magnificent and awe-inspiring; it looked indeed as if it but yesterday had boiled up out of chaos. There were peaks rising abruptly from the gorges that were nothing but masses of huge and polished stones indubitably ejected when California was in her throes. The longer sweeps of the mountain range were dark with primordial forest. True, the way lay along the edge of precipices and Aleece shrieked every time the horses slipped over the edge or we met a team on the narrow road, but there is always something.

35

We arrived in Santa Barbara so coated with dust, looking so dehumanized, so altogether disreputable, that the haughty clerk of the Arlington Hotel was about to turn us away, inferring we must be nobodies to have travelled by stage instead of luxurious train; when I suddenly remembered that my father-in-law had once been a landholder in the county and shamelessly invoked his name. We were shown at once to a comfortable suite.

The De la Guerras were my objective in Santa Barbara, for of all the families of Old California theirs had been the most notable, not excepting the Castros, Alvarados, and Arguellos. Don José de la Guerra, a descendant of Spanish grandees, had migrated from Mexico in the latter part of the eighteenth century with a grant of three hundred thousand Departmental acres in his pocket. Thousands of cattle roamed his ranches and he did an extensive trade in hides with the Boston skippers. He was the leading figure in such politics as there were, and the house in Santa Barbara—Casa Grande—was the scene of constant and magnificent hospitality. It was in this famous old mansion that Alfred Robinson had married a daughter of the house, a ceremony immortalized by Richard Henry Dana in *Two Years Before the Mast*. The splendor had continued for a time under his son, Don Pablo, but the American adventurers with their sharp practices had gradually denuded him of his acres, and today there was little left to his widow and her three children, Carlos, Delfina, and Herminia. The eldest daughter, Mrs. Dibblee, had married a wealthy Bostonian, and lived in a large stone house on a bluff overhanging the Channel, for long the finest private residence in Southern California.

This time I had taken the precaution to bring a letter of introduction, for although I was determined to be taken into Casa Grande, the De la Guerras were not a family one could walk in upon and from whom demand a lodging.

* * *

Santa Barbara was not the modern and almost oppressively wealthy city it is today, and the Mexican driver of the lone street car would obligingly halt and let one run into a drug store for an ice cream soda while he lolled on his stool and smoked the eternal cigarette; but it was sufficiently puzzling with its houses almost hidden behind their luxuriant shrubbery and often surrounded by hedges as impenetrable as walls. When, bathed, shampooed, fed, we set forth to find Casa Grande, we were obliged to ask our way several times before we reached the old Spanish Plaza on which it was situated, not far from the blue waters of the Channel, but almost obscured by the American mushrooms overlapping it.

Casa Grande lay about three sides of a courtyard, a graceful structure of one story, painted white under a roof of red tiles. I approached the wide front door facing the square with some trepidation. The friend in Monterey who had given me the note of introduction had told me the De la Guerras were very proud—and the Spanish can be prouder than any race on earth—and no doubt would be horrified at the bare suggestion of taking lodgers into that sacrosanct mansion. I would have to use the utmost tact.

I had handed the maid my note of introduction, and in a few moments Señora de la Guerra and her daughters Delfina and Herminia entered and gave us a hospitable if ceremonious welcome. The señora spoke no English. Herminia, recently widowed, looked sad and distrait. I felt that my best hope lay with Delfina. She was a quite lovely young woman with dark hair and Spanish green eyes that twinkled understandingly. I guessed she knew quite well what I was after, for she must have been prepared for our visit by her friends in Monterey. I determined to place my cards on the table at once, and told her frankly that I had the vague outlines of a novel in mind, whose scene was Santa Barbara, and more particularly Casa Grande. It was a great deal to ask, I knew, but if there *was* a spare bedroom, and if she *would* let us have it, we'd promise to give no trouble at all.

It was evident they had talked the matter over, for, after a rapid conversation in Spanish with her mother, Delfina led us to a room at the extreme end of one of the wings. It was a large airy room, cleaner and better furnished than any that had been our lot hitherto, but that was a mere nothing beside the information that it had once been occupied by

Concepción (Concha) Arguello, heroine of the one famous love story of Old California; when, after Rezenov had sailed away never to return, she had assumed the habit of the third order of Franciscans and devoted her life to good works. It was years before I wrote *Rezenov* but it was always in the back of my mind.

The result of those weeks in Santa Barbara was *The Doomswoman*, a short novel inspired by that atmosphere of the past and something of Delfina's personality.

Delfina and Herminia danced the old Spanish dances for me, showed me the costumes, shawls, mantillas, worn by their more fortunate ancestors; and Mrs. Dibblee, a regal woman who retained all the tender grace of her girlhood despite a large family, told me many incidents in the history of the De la Guerras. She also entertained us at her house on the cliff and took us for long drives; even Aleece enjoyed that visit to Santa Barbara. "Rather different from those greasy old relics you tried to get inspiration out of," she commented dryly. "You'd never take the De la Guerras for anything but what they are, and it's a relief to walk about in a civilized town once more, not a collection of mud hovels."

The Mission, the only one at that time in a state of complete repair, dominated the town from rising ground in the east, and with its brown-robed Franciscans must have looked much as it did in the old days when the padres were all-powerful in California. The priests were very genial; they entertained us at luncheon, and took us up to one of the belfries where we had a magnificent view of the riotous color of the valley, the ripe fruit in the orchards, the deep sapphire blue of the Channel. Above, the unflecked sky was as blue as the water, and behind the Mission the rocky frowning mountains rose in almost perpendicular lines, strangely barren and bleak in contrast with the luxuriance at their feet.

Delfina conceived the idea of having an old time *merienda* (picnic) in a rocky gorge, as one of her many contributions to "atmosphere," but as I sat down on a snake other memories of that festivity are somewhat hazy.

From Santa Barbara we went to Los Angeles, a town of some fifty thousand inhabitants, shabby and sleepy.

*Edward Selden Spaulding (1891-1982) served as headmaster of La-
guna Blanca School from its founding in 1933 until 1953. This story
is one of his tales of Santa Barbara ranch life between 1875 and 1925.*

THE SILVER
MOUNTED SADDLE

OLD ALFREDO WAS in an expansive mood. Mary and I had ridden up to the Quemada to enjoy a quiet picnic beside the tiny spring there and, finding the vaquero already there when we arrived, we had shared our lunch with him. Now, with the sandwiches eaten and the little fire over which he had made our coffee burned out, we were reclining comfortably in the pleasant shade of the madronos.

"This is a pleasant country," observed the vaquero.

"It is a beautiful country," replied Mary. "This was Mother Williams' favorite spot on the Ranch. She came up here often before she was hurt in the runaway. And I love it as much as she did."

"I was born here," observed Old Alfredo reminiscently and pointedly, also. "That was long ago."

"Up here on the Quemada?" asked Mary, humoring the old man's mood even though she knew the story well.

"Oh sure, right here," he said again. "My father built a little house up here. That was before the big fire burned that place all out, so there ain't nothing left to show where it was exactly. That was a very long time ago. Many years before you was born, Mary."

"Tell us about it," said Mary.

"Oh, no, Mary," replied Old Alfredo. "It is a very long story. The Patrón has heard it many times, and he wants me to work, not to tell stories. No, Patrón?"

"Tell us again, Alfredo," said I lazily. "I am very comfortable here. It is a very pleasant day. And this is an interesting story. Tell it again to us."

The old man rolled a cigarette as he brought his thoughts together. When he was ready, he began his tale.

"In the old days, long ago, things were different from what they is now," he stated.

"How were they different, Alfredo?"

"They was very different," stated the old vaquero positively. "There was only adobe to build houses with, and so there was only little houses. There was no casas grandes. Santa Barbara was a little town. There were no streets. Every man built his adobe wherever it suited him, and the trails ran in and out and around. The Padre was the big shot. Oh, there was the Governor, of course, and one or two others; but there was no lawyers, no doctors, just the ordinary paisanos and a few who owned ranchos. There was no watches and no clocks. There was a calendar, I guess; but nobody paid any attention to it. There was just the rainy season and the dry season, and Spring was in between. There was no money."

"There must have been some money," said I.

"Oh, sure; maybe there was some money, but not much. We didn't have none."

"What happened when someone became sick?" inquired Mary.

"Oh, he got well or he died," said the old man without emotion. "That is what happens now, ain't it? Only now, there is the doctor in between. All the women knew about taking care of sick people. There was good plants that they used to find in the canyons and on the hillsides. Maybe, the Priest said a blessing. People wasn't sick much.

"In those days, the Ruiz boys used to run their cattle in the canyons back of the Old Mission and Montecito. Not many. Just a few. Just enough

40

to give them some fresh meat once and a-while. The Padres had the big bunches. They had very many, so many nobody ever bothered to count them. Some of them was so wild they was like deer. And if once and a while one of the Ruiz boys took one of these broncos, who cared? What difference did it make? Those wild fellahs was dangerous. It was very hard to take one. But them three Ruiz boys was very quick and very smart, and they had good horses; so it was all right.

"The youngest of these Ruiz boys was my father, and he was tall and light and young, and he had a fine mustache. He was handsome, and his hands and feet were small. He wasn't big like you, Billee. He was a good roper, too, much better than me, now. Yes, with a riata he was very good. Once he roped and killed a bear all alone. Yes sir, he did! Oh, he was very bravo. And with the señoritas, too! He rode a silver mounted saddle that he won in Los Angeles one time when they had a big fiesta there. The Governor was there and he put up a fine saddle with a lot of silver conchos on it for the best rider and roper. It was a very big time. And my father won it. Yes sir, he won it against everybody."

"He couldn't have been a better roper than you are, Alfredo," murmured Mary.

"Well, he was very good," said the old vaquero. "And he was very proud of that saddle. How do you say it? It meant something special to him."

"It was a symbol, I guess," said I.

"Maybe so. One day my father, this Charley Ruiz, got all dressed up for town. He put this saddle on his best horse and he rode down the canyon to see his sweetheart. He was feeling fine. He swung with the swing of his horse under him. He listened to the jingle of his long spur chains and the roll of the wheel of the bit on his horse's tongue. You know how it is when a fellah is young, Billee!"

"I know very well," cried Mary. "Didn't I see Will come riding down Chapala Street just before we were married?"

"He crossed the creek where the stone bridge is now," continued Alfredo. "And he rode through the big arch in the wall, the stone wall that used to be there before they put the road up the canyon.

"At the Mission, there was Father Peter standing on the front step. Charley was no great church-goer, he was too much of a *caballero* for that; but it was Father Peter, who was going to marry him some day; so he had to keep on the good side of the Priest. He reined in his horse and greeted Father Peter politely. They talked about this and that, about the cattle, about Charley not coming to Mass as often as the Priest thought he should come, about Charley getting married pretty soon and settling down. You know what a Priest would talk about!

"Pretty soon, as they talked, another young fellah, an Americano, rode by on a gray horse and went on up the canyon, This American had come to Santa Barbara on one of the ships. He was a sailor. When this foreigner rode by, Charley forgot about the Priest and what he was saying; and he watched this fellah till he disappeared up the canyon. That is a good horse, Charley thought. Iron-grays is quick and tough. They make good horses with the cattle. But this man, this Americano —"

Old Alfredo shrugged his shoulders expressively as he left the sentence unfinished and hanging in the air.

"Who was this Americano?" asked Mary quickly.

"*Quién sabe!*" said Alfredo without interest. "He was just a sailor. I never was told his name. What difference does it make?"

"Go ahead with the story, Alfredo," said I. "Tell us what happened next."

"Well my father let the Priest talk on," continued the vaquero. Priests like to talk. My father looked off, down to the ocean and then across. There was the Islands and Mt. Diablo sticking up just as it does now. Pretty soon, he says *adiós* to Father Peter and he rode down into the town to the house of his sweetheart. Inez lived down there somewhere near where De la Guerra Street now is. She came out of her house and talked to him. For a-while, he didn't get off his horse because he wanted to show off his silver saddle. She stood at his bridle rein and talked to him."

"Tell us about her, Alfredo," said Mary. "She was going to be your mother, wasn't she? Was she very lovely?"

"Oh yes, she was very beautiful. She was fourteen, maybe fifteen. She was — How do you call it, Billee? *Muchísima dulce?*"

"Oh, very sweet, very lovely," I said.

"She was the most beautiful girl in all of Santa Barbara. My father looked down at her from his silver saddle and he thought what a lucky *caballero* he was to have her for his girl. Then he thought of the sailor fellah, who had been hanging around Inez's house, too. Inez's father didn't like Charley so good. He says a beautiful girl like Inez was should catch somebody better than Charley, some *ranchero*, maybe. The mother sided with Charley because he was young and because he had a fine mustache. That silver mounted saddle meant something to the *señoras* and the *señoritas*. So Charley was upset."

"'When are we going to get married?' he asks her. 'Oh, some day this Summer; or perhaps later,' she told him. 'What is the hurry, Charley? We are young. We are happy. Why not stay this way for awhile!'"

"Charley didn't like this very much. He argued with Inez, but she was young and she was happy and she wouldn't come down to business. She smiled and showed Charley how beautiful she was. Pretty soon, Charley got mad and rode away. If he had met this sailor fellah then, there would have been a fight and somebody would have got hurt. There was no policemen walking up and down the streets then to stop a fight.

"The next time that my father saw this girl of his, things was even worse. She smiled at him, all right but, underneath, she — she — I don't know how to say it. My father thought she was playing with him."

"Was she coy with him?" suggested Mary. "She led him on, perhaps, and at the same time, she let him feel that her thoughts were with someone else?"

"Yes, that was it," said the old man. "She smiled at him and she teased him and she wouldn't come down to business. She made my father so mad that, pretty soon, he rode off to town and had a drink or two with some of his friends. After a-while, he started back to his adobe in the canyon; and he went by way of Inez's house. Maybe, he thought he would stop and argue with her some more. Maybe, he was a little drunk. I don't know how it was. He rode by the house, and there was this gray horse standing at the hitching post. So that was it! That made Charley very mad! He reined in his horse, thinking that he would go into the house and kill this sailor, this foreigner. Oh, he was very bravo! Then he thought no, there is plenty of other girls in town. Let him have her. A girl that likes these foreigners is no good, anyhow. And so he dug his spurs into his horse and went galloping toward the Mission.

"He stayed away for a week. Then, one evening, he got all dressed up and rode down to her house again. 'Are you going to marry me?' he asks as soon as he sees her, 'or ain't you?'"

"'I don't know,' she tells him. 'Why did you ride away so angrily the other day? That wasn't very polite of you. Maybe, you don't want to marry me any more. Maybe, you got some other girl now!'"

"'Of course I want to marry you, Inez,' cries my father. 'Why do you talk that way? You didn't used to do it. You keep putting me off all the time. What is the matter?'"

"'I'm not putting you off, Charley,' says the girl. 'I am very happy. Why do we hurry into something we don't know very much about? Let's wait till we are sure.'"

"'I am sure,' cries Charley bitterly, 'but you ain't! That's the trouble. You ain't sure you want me. Maybe, another fellah on a gray horse has come riding along.'"

"My father began to get mad again. He was a very quick-tempered fellah."

"'I'll tell you something, Inez,' he says furiously. 'You won't never marry no one else but me. I'll take care of that other fellah.'"

"'Charley,' cries the girl, 'I love you when you talk like that. You look so fierce and handsome! Why ain't you always that way? Is it because, sometimes, you love me more; or is it because, sometimes, you get a little jealous and want to fight somebody? When you are cold and cross and ride away mad, then I don't love you at all. Here is my scarf. Wear it tomorrow when you ride at the Estero.'"

"That night, my father rode back to his house in the canyon with his head in the clouds. Young men is like that when their girls smile at them. Inez had set the wedding day in September, and the old man had agreed to it. It was June now. September would be here soon. My father sang in the starlight as he rode up the trail.

"The next day, there was a big fiesta in the town and everybody had a good time. In the afternoon, they all went to the Estero to have some fun, riding and roping and pulling each other off their horses. Charley was very good at these things and he was sure he would win the prize. It was a pair of silver spurs. They would go good with his fine saddle, he figured.

"It was a big time. There was judges and girls and the old *vaqueros* and everybody. While Charley was waiting for his turn to come around, a little thing happened that stuck in his head afterwards: A dog trotted out to the middle of the place where the *vaqueros* were working. It was a pretty big dog. It was dangerous because, any time, it could run under a running horse's feet and throw him. Men whistled and shouted and cussed at the dog, but it wouldn't come. Dogs are like that sometimes. One of the judges tried to ride it off the field, but he was an old man and he was on an old, steady horse and couldn't get nowhere. At last, two young *vaqueros*, with their riatas swinging around their heads and making a big show for the girls, came out of the crowd on the run. They threw almost together. One caught the dog by the neck and the other by the hind quarters. Then the horses flared apart and the rope snapped tight. The dog's head was jerked right off."

"'Bravo, Hernandez! Bravo, Romero!' cries my father as the two *vaqueros* comes riding in with the dog's body dragging behind them in the dirt. 'Well done,' he says."

"When my father's turn comes, he's done fine. Oh, he was very good. He roped the big, wild animal as slick as grease; but when he tried to throw him, his cinch broke and he got a bad fall. And so he didn't win anything."

"That was a brutal thing to do to that poor dog." interrupted Mary. "Did the spectators enjoy that, Alfredo?"

"Oh sure, they liked it. It was very slick," said the old vaquero. "Those boys could rope in those days."

"How could they like it?" cried Mary, very much upset. "The girls and women and the older men? They didn't like it, Alfredo!"

"Oh sure, they liked it fine," insisted the old man. "You wouldn't like it, Mary; but they liked it fine. Things was different in those days. People wasn't so nice. They wasn't so — so — I don't know how you say it. They lived — you say it for me, Billee."

"They lived simpler lives closer to nature, I guess," I said.

"Maybe so," said Old Alfredo, thinking deeply. "There wasn't no doctors then, or no lawyers. There wasn't no books. There was no play-acting. The paisanos butchered their own meat, and the women did it, too, sometimes. Life and death was all around them."

"Let's get back to Charley Ruiz," I suggested. "What happened to him and to Inez after the cinch broke and he didn't win the spurs?"

"His name wasn't really Charley, was it, Alfredo?" asked Mary.

"No, it wasn't," agreed the vaquero. "It was Carlos. But pretty soon, you people began to call him Charley, and then, pretty soon, everybody began to call him Charley. Charley Ruiz. Everybody knew Charley Ruiz."

"Go ahead with the story," I suggested again.

"The next couple of months was no good for Charley," said the old man, picking up the story again under my urging. "Maybe, he broke something inside of him. He was stiff and very sore. He couldn't get on his horse for a long time. He was discouraged. He had lost the spurs and he thought he was losing his girl, and he hurt like Hell inside. Everything was no good for him.

"Then he began to get better. Pretty soon, he was riding a little. Not much, just a little! Then there was the big doings at the Alamar Ranch, just outside of town, a barbecue and dancing and things like that, and Charley went to it. Inez and Charley's two brothers was there. Everybody was there. The sailor on the gray horse was there. It was a big party, a big party.

"Charley watched Inez very close. Sometimes she smiled at him. Sometimes she smiled at the sailor, this *Americano*. You know how girls is. Charley couldn't be sure. Then he missed her. He looked all around for her but he couldn't find her. Pretty soon, he met his brother, Juan.

"'Have you seen her, Juan?'" he says to his brother.

"'She went for a walk with the sailor in the moonlight,' Juan told him. 'I seen them start up the road. I think we got to take care of this foreigner, Carlos.'"

46

"This made my father very mad. Oh very mad!"

"'I'm going to settle this business,' he told his brother. "You stay around where I can find you, Juan.'"

"My father went over to his horse and put everything ready. Then he started up the road in the moonlight. He was very *bravo*, very bad. And Juan went along, too.

"Pretty soon he seen them walking very slow in the road ahead of him, and he punched his spurs into his horse.

"The girl heard him coming, and she turned her head to see who it was. She screamed and the sailor started to run. He was crazy."

"Why was he crazy, Alfredo?" asked Mary. "He was afraid."

"To run up a road from a *vaquero* with a *riata* in his hand?" cried Alfredo, his eyes afire. "Sure he was crazy."

"What should he have done?" I asked.

"Nothing! There was nothing that he could do. Unless there was a tree handy. But then what good is a tree with a man on both sides of it?"

For a moment the old *vaquero* was silent as he relived this most important incident of his father's life. Then he resumed his tale.

"Charley dropped the loop of his *riata* over the sailor's head just like that. That was all there was to it. Inez was scared. She stood there and watched my father drag the sailor away. After a while, he came riding back. He was leading the gray horse.

"'Well,' said my father, looking down at her from his saddle.

"'Did you kill him, Charley?' she asked, very scared.

"'No! You did,' said my father."

"He got down from his horse slowly. He still was stiff and sore, and it was hard work."

"'Get up in my saddle,' he ordered the girl."

"'Get up,' was all he said."

"He helped the girl up into the silver saddle, and then he got up on the gray horse.

"That's how my father and mother happened to come up here to the Quemada. That's how I was born up here. That was a long time ago."

"What happened to the sailor?" I asked. "Wasn't there some trouble about him?"

"What trouble could there be?" demanded Old Alfredo scornfully. "Who cared anything about this foreigner, this sailor, this *Americano!*"

"There must have been some talk," declared Mary. "Somebody must have asked questions about him. What about Father Peter? He must have had something to say about you and Inez and where this sailor had disappeared to."

"Who cared!" demanded the son of Charley Ruiz indignantly. "Not the priest. The priest didn't care where he was. This heretic! Oh, maybe he gave Inez a little penance to do when she went to confession later. You know how these priests are. But not much. And the Alcalde, what did he care about this sailor, this trouble maker? Everybody was glad to have him disappear. Nobody asked no questions.

"That's how my father and mother came to live up here," said the old man, finishing his story, "and they liked it fine. My father built a little shack right here by this spring and they lived in it for five years or so. Maybe, longer! I liked it fine, too. I still come up here once and a-while and look around."

KATE SANBORN

Kate Sanborn (1839-1917) was a popular writer, observant and witty, author of several humorous books, who set out to see California for herself. She reported her findings in A Truthful Woman in Southern California *(1893). One of the highlights of the trip was her stay in Santa Barbara.*

IN GALA DRESS

"The sun is warm, the sky is clear,
The waves are dancing, fast and bright;
Both isles and snowy mountains wear
The purple noon's transparent light."

TO SEE SANTA BARBARA at its best you must go there for the Floral Carnival. Then at high noon, on a mid-April day, all State Street is brilliantly decorated with leaves of the date-palm, pampa plumes, moss combined with tropical foliage, calla-lilies, wild-flowers, bamboo, immortelles, branches of pepper trees, evergreens, lemon boughs laden with yellow fruit, and variegated shrubs. Draperies of white and gold, with green or red in contrast, or blue and white, in harmony with red flowers, of floral arches draped with fish-nets bestrewn with pink roses; or yellow alone in draperies combined with the poppy, or gray moss and roses. No one fails to respond to the color summons for the day of days. The meat-markets are tastefully concealed with a leafy screen and callas. The undertaker makes his place as cheerful as possible with evergreens, roses, and red geraniums. The drugstore is gaily trimmed, and above the door see the great golden mortar made of marigolds. The Mexican and Californian colors are often flung out, and flags are flying from many windows. The long broad street is a blaze of glory; the immense audience, seated on tiers of benches, wait patiently, then impatiently, for the expected procession; and as many more people are standing in line, equally eager. Many have baskets or armfuls of flowers, with which to pelt the passing acquaintance. There are moments of such intense interest that everything is indelibly and eternally photographed. I see, as I write, the absolutely cloudless sky of perfect blue, the sea of darker shade, equally perfect, the white paved street, the kaleidoscope of color, the fluttering pennants, the faces of the crowd all turned in one direction, and hark! the band is really coming the beginning of the pageant is just seen, and now sea, sky, flags, crowds are no more regarded, for the long-talked-of parade is here. See advancing the Grand Commander and his showy aids, gay Spanish cavaliers, the horses stepping proudly, realizing the importance of the occasion, the saddles and bridles wound with ribbons or covered with flowers. And next the Goddess of Flowers, in canopy-covered shell, a pretty little Mayflower of a maiden, with a band of maids of honor, each in a dainty shell. The shouts and applause add to the excitement, and flowers are hurled in merry war at the cavaliers, and the goddess and her attendants. Next comes the George Washington coach, modelled after the historic vehicle, occupied by stately dames and courtly gentlemen in colonial array; even the footmen are perfection in the regulation livery of that period. Solemn and imposing this may be, but they get a merciless shower of roses, and one of the prizes. And do look at the haymakers! Oh, that is charming! Country girls and boys on a load of new-mown hay, with broad-brimmed hats, and dresses trimmed with wild-flowers. And now the advance-guard is coming down again; they have just turned at the head of the line, and it is already a little confusing. But the judges! How can they keep cool, or even think, with such a clamor of voices, and guests chattering thoughtlessly to them. Here comes a big basket on wheels, handle and all covered with moss and roses. Four girls in pink silk trimmed with moss stand within, bearing shields of pink roses to protect their laughing faces from excess attention. What a lovely picture! Another basket just behind covered entirely with marguerites; the wheels also are each a marguerite, the white horses with harness covered with yellow ribbon—so dainty, so cool. Is it better than the other? And here is a Roman chariot, a Spanish market-wagon, a phaeton covered with yellow mustard, a hermit in monastic garb; then Robin Hood and his merry men, and Maid Marian in yellow-green habit, Will Scarlet and Friar Tuck in green doublets, yellow facings, bright green felt hats, bows and quivers flower-trimmed, even the tiny arrows winged with blossoms. Now there are equipages three deep to survey instead of one, as they pass and repass in bewildering splendor. And do look! Here come the comicalities! "The Old Woman who lived in a Shoe"—a big floral slipper, with a dozen children in pink and gray-green, and the old woman on great poke-bonnet; a Japanese jinrikisha; and egg of white flowers, and a little boy hid away so as to peep and put out a downy head as a yellow chicken; a bicycle brigade; equestriennes; and an interesting procession of native Californians, with the accoutrements of the Castilian, on horseback. One carriage is banked with marigolds, and the black horses are harnessed in yellow of the exact shade. It is fitly occupied by black-eyed Spanish beauties, with raven hair done up high with gold combs, and black lace costumes with marigolds for trimming, and takes a well-deserved prize.

Roses, roses, roses, roses! How they fly and fall as the fleeting display is passing! Thirty thousand on one carriage. Roses cover the street. And yet the gardens don't seem stripped. Where millions are blooming thousands are not missed. And not roses alone, but every flower of field and garden and conservatory is honored and displayed. Now the contestants are driving up to the grand stand to secure silken banners. Every one looks a little bit weary in procession and audience. Is it over? I murmur regretfully:

> "All that's bright must fade,
> The brightest still the fleetest;
> And that's sweet was made
> But to be lost when sweetest."

Yes, it is over! Waving banners, rainbow colors, showers of blossoms, rosy faces, mimic battle, fairy scenes, the ideal realized!

This is better than the New Orleans Mardi Gras, so often marred by rain and mud, with mythological ambiguities that few can understand, and difficult to interpret in passing tableaux; better than similar display at Nice and Mentone. This I do call "unique" and the only. Let Santa Barbara have this yearly fiesta for her own. She has fairly won the competition.

We at the comparatively frozen and prosaic north can indulge in gay coaching parades at Franconia, Newport, or Lenox, where costumes of gorgeous hues assist the natural beauty of the flowers. But it is only a coaching parade, at the wind-up of a gay season. We cannot catch the evanescent glamour, the optical enchantment, the fantastic fun, the exquisite art of making long preparation and hard work, careful schemes for effect, appear like airy nonsense for the amusement of an idle hour. We show the machinery. A true carnival can only be a success in a perpetual "Summer-land," "within a lovely landscape on a bright and laughing seacoast." Taine said, "Give me the race, the surroundings, and the epoch, and I show you the man." Give me fair women, roses, sunshine, leisure, and high-bred, prancing steeds, and I show you this Santa Barbara Carnival.

But this is only a portion of the entertainment. There is a display of flowers at the Pavilion, where everything can be found that blooms in California, all most artistically arrayed; and more fascinating in the evening, when hundreds of tiny electric lights twinkle everywhere from out the grayish-green moss, and the hall is filled with admiring guests. There is always a play given one evening by amateur talent, a tournament, and a grand closing ball.

The tournament is exciting, where skilful riders try tilting at rings, trying to take as many rings as possible on lance while galloping by the wires on which these rings are lightly suspended—a difficult accomplishment. Their costumes are elaborate and gay, but never outre or bizarre, and no two alike. Each has his own color, and, like the knights of old, has a fayre ladye among the spectators who is especially interested and anxious for his success.

Next comes the Spanish game of *colgar*, picking up ten-dollar gold pieces from the saddle, the horse at full speed. And the gymkhana race ends the games. Those who enter, saddle at the word "Go," open an umbrella, and, taking out a cigar, light and smoke it—then see who first rides to the goal.

Last came the real vaqueros, and they rid untamed, unbroken horses, after a long and rather painful struggle to mount. They lasso mustangs and do wonderful things. But it was too much. I was glad to go and rest.

The Flower Dance at the ball, where human flowers formed intricate figures and dances of our edification and delight, was so attractive that my words are of no avail. Picture twenty-eight young ladies, each dressed to represent a flower—hollyhock, pansy, moss, rose, morning-glory, eucalyptus, blossom, pink clover, yellow marguerite, Cherokee rose, pink carnation, forget-me-not, buttercup, pink-and-white fuchsia, lily of the valley, wine-colored peony, white iris, daffodil, and so on. They advance with slowly swaying motion, with wreaths uplifted until they reach the stage, where sit the guests of honor. There they bow low, then lay the garlands at their feet, and retire, forming ingeniously pretty groups and figures, while bees and butterflies flit in and out. See the bees pursuing the little pink rosebuds until at last they join hands and dance gaily away, only to be enthusiastically recalled.

Do you ladies want to understand a little in detail about the dresses? Of course you do. Well, here is the yellow marguerite:

Slender petals of yellow satin falling over a skirt of white silk crepe, a green satin calyx girdle about her waist, and golden petals drooped again from the neck of her low bodice and over her shoulders.

A handsome brunette represented a wine-colored peony in a rich costume of wine-colored velvet and satin. The petals fell to make the skirt, and rose again from a bell sheathing the neck of her low corsage, and the cap on her dark hair was a copy of the flower.

There, you see how it is done. But it requires genius to succeed in such an undertaking. Look at Walter Crane's pictures of human flowers for more suggestions.

Most effective of all was the cachuca, danced by a girl of pure Castilian blood, who was dressed to symbolize the scarlet passion-flower. The room was darkened save where she stood, and her steps and poses were full of Spanish fire and feeling, combined with poetic grace.

Yes, it is over, but the pictures remain as freshly colored as if I saw it all but yesterday.

During the Carnival sentiment reigns supreme—that is, if you have engaged rooms far in advance, and the matter of three daily meals is settled—and portly business men become gallant, chivalrous, and even poetic. In testimony I offer two verses sent to a lady visitor with a bunch of roses:

"We had not thought it was for aught
He lingered round us, scanning
But to admire our spring attire,
The south wind softly fanning.

"But when we knew it was for you
Our charms he sought to capture,
All round the bower each budding flower
Blushed pink with rosy rapture.

"Lovingly,

THE ROSES."

George Eliot once said: "You love the roses—so do I! I wish the sky would rain down roses as they rain from all the shaken bush. Why will it not? Then all the valleys would be pink and white, and soft to tread on. They would fall as light as feathers, smelling sweet; and it would be like sleeping and yet waking all at once."

She never knew Santa Barbara.

I said the horses feel proud, and their owners tell me how they turn their heads to see their adornment, And well they may, for a true Barbareno loves his horse as does the Arab, and delights in his decoration. Easily first in this matter is Mr. W. D. Thompson, who came to Santa Barbara from Maine more than forty years ago, a nephew of the captain with whom Dana sailed. Mr. Thompson is a progressive man, who appreciates the many improvements achieved and contemplated, but still loves to tell of the good old times when he was roughing it as a pioneer. He has done a most important and valuable work in having a typical Mexican saddle and bridle of the most approved and correct pattern made out of the finest leather and several thousand silver dollars. As his favorite mare stood before me with his magnificent saddle on, and her forelegs tied with a little strap so that she could step daintily but not run, I never saw such a pretty sight of the kind. This saddle and bridle, worth over $3000, are now on exhibition in Chicago. No more significant or beautiful exhibition of the early argonautic period could be sent from Southern California, and it will surely attract constant and admiring attention. Here is a description from the San Francisco Argonaut:

Everybody up and down the coast knows Dixie Thompson. His talk is full of delightful anecdotes of the early settlers, and he has a droll, dry humor of his own that is refreshing. Mr. Nordhoff, who is an old friend, once wrote to the *Harper* "Drawer" about his shrewd way of restraining the over-keen traders and laboring men who tried to impose upon him. He headed the pleasant bit of gossip, "Captain Thompson's Club," and says:

> "Captain Dixie is, to all appearance, the man of most leisure in all leisurely Santa Barbara. He and his horses and carriages are always at the service of a friend. But while he seems to be the idlest of men, he is, in fact, an extremely capable business man who has many irons in the fire—tills much good land, has horses and cattle and pigs of the best breeds on many hills and in several rich valleys, and keeps all his affairs running in good order. Still, he is an easy-going, not a bustling, man of business. And it is just here that his social contrivance comes in: he has judged it expedient to form a club.

"'You see,' said he, the other day, to an old friend, 'the boys don't always see me around, and sometimes they try to take a little advantage. I find a fellow who don't haul half a load for me while I am paying for a full load; another one who gives me short measure; or another who does not do what I have told him. I hate to scold; and as they all deny when I accuse them, and I can't be telling men that they are lying to me, I though I'd just establish a Liars' Club and bring them all in. It is now in good, healthy operation. We don't call it the Liars' Club, of course; we speak of the Club. But when I catch a man trying to 'do' me, I just tell him that I'll have to make him a member of the Club.—Oh, how do you do, Mr. President?' said Captain Dixie to a well-known character just then passing by.—'He's the president of the Club, you know,' he added. 'Here's Pancho now; I told him the other day I would have to make him a member of the Club if he didn't look out. I guess he'll get in yet. It's a very flourishing club, and more useful, I guess, than some others.

"Don't laugh, my dear Drawer. I believe Captain Thompson has struck an admirable idea, and one which might well have wide application. Don't you suppose the material for such a club exists, for instance—not here in New Haven, of course, but over in New York, say, or perhaps in Washington? Think it over. The Drawer has always taken the lead in great moral and social improvements. I leave it to you."

Here, as in all Southern California, you will never know anything of the real town unless you have a friend who can take you to unfrequented cross-country drives up winding paths to mesas, or upland pasture guarded by lock and key from the average tourist, and get views indescribably fine.

I am ashamed of my fellow-travellers who pick oranges by the score, and even break off boughs from the choicest and most conspicuous trees, and rush uninvited pell-mell into private grounds, and quiet homes of well-bred people to see and exclaim and criticize. Add to this nuisance the fact that hundreds of invalids come yearly to the most desirable localities, turning them into camping grounds for bacilli. I wonder at the singular forbearance and courtesy of the residents.

Occasionally someone invited to speechify or air his opinion of things in general here bluntly expresses his surprise at finding everywhere so much culture, wealth, and refinement. This is a queer reflection of the fact that this part of the State is filled with specimens of our finest families from the East. I will frankly admit that I must be at my very best to keep up with those I have been privileged to meet here.

You must not forget when in Santa Barbara to visit the fine public library, the best adapted for the convenience of actual workers of any I have entered. You must not fail to drive to Montecito ("little forest"), to Carpinteria and Goleta.

I also advise you to spend a morning in Mr. Ford's studio, and an afternoon with Mr. Starke and his treasures in wood-carving and inlaying, brought yearly from the Yosemite, wrought out with his own hands. He uses nearly fifty varieties of trees in his woodwork, and few see his stock and go away without investing in a redwood cane, a paper-knife, or an inlaid table. His orders come from all parts of the world, and are often very large, mounting up to hundreds of dollars. He is a simple-hearted student of nature, and a thorough workman. I enjoyed a brief visit to Chinatown and Spanishtown close by, where I saw a woman scrubbing clothes on a long flat board, with a piece of soap in each hand, standing in a hut made of poles covered with brush, and noticed an old oven outdoors and the meat hung up in strips to dry. I enjoyed also a call on the old fellow who "catcha de fisha."

And now, looking back as we are whirled away, I find I am repeating those lines from Shelley which so exactly reproduce the picture:

> "The earth and ocean seem
>   To sleep in one another's arms and dream
>   Of waves, flowers, clouds, woods, rocks, and all that we
>   Read in their smiles, and call reality."

SANTA BARBARA

Between the mountains and the sea,
    Walled by the rock, fringed by the foam,
A valley stretches fair and free
    Beneath the blue of heaven's dome.

At rest in that fair valley lies
    Saint Barbara, the beauteous maid;
Above her head the cloudless skies
    Smile down upon her charms displayed.

The sunlit mountains o'er her shed
    The splendor of their purple tinge;
While round her, like a mantle, spread,
    The blue seas with their silver fringe.

Enfolded in that soothing calm,
    The earth seems sweet, and heaven near;
The flowers bloom free, the air is balm,
    And summer rules the radiant year.

Francis Fisher Browne
— *1897*

58

MARSHALL BOND, JR.

Marshall Bond, Jr. (1908-1983) was a life-long resident of Santa Barbara, a businessman, environmentalist and enthusiast of western Americana. The author of several books, the best is the charming autobi-ography, Adventures with Peons, Princes & Tycoons *(1983). In it he wrote fondly of his Santa Barbara boyhood.*

AROUND THE UPPER EAST

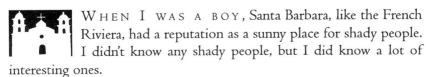 W HEN I WAS A BOY, Santa Barbara, like the French Riviera, had a reputation as a sunny place for shady people. I didn't know any shady people, but I did know a lot of interesting ones.

Actually I was born in the Good Samaritan Hospital in Los Angeles. My father remarked at the time I resembled a hunk of fishbait. In spite of this, I prospered and even moved to Santa Barbara two weeks later which I have always considered was the smartest thing I ever did.

Formerly my family had been living in Seattle but, because of my mother's health, usually spent the winters in California and, in 1914, bought a home at 328 East Islay Street in Santa Barbara. My mother occupied it for forty years. Santa Barbara was then a town of some fifteen thousand inhabitants and few paved streets. It was surrounded by cattle and citrus ranches and several million acres of glorious wilderness — the Los Padres National Forest, where we often went camping.

One of my earliest experiences was working as an extra in the movies. The American Film Company had been established in 1913 and had built a studio shortly thereafter on the corner of State and Mission Street called The Flying A. Francis X. Bushman, Wallace Reid, and Mary Miles Minter were among the early stars, and Henry King and William Desmond Taylor were prominent directors.

59

Nearby was a western set which consisted of store fronts propped up by just enough timbers to prevent them from collapsing. After school my friends and I often visited this ghost town which came to life when a western was being filmed. We mingled with the extras and, on one occasion, the director asked me to run up to the leading lady and present her with a bouquet of flowers. For this performance I received the princely remuneration of a package of chewing gum. My career as an occasional extra in the movies lasted for about three years.

A thrilling melodrama, The Secret of the Submarine, was ground out every week in a large tank at the rear of the studio. The hero of this spectacular was Tom Chatterton, who lived next door to us, raised Rhode Island Red chickens, and had a wife he called "Dearie." Tom and Dearie would have been ideal neighbors except for the early morning crowing of their big red rooster which they refused to get rid of even though it greatly irritated my father.

When we had the price of tickets to the Mission Theatre my school friends and I would sit spellbound on Saturday afternoon watching Tom Chatterton, the captain of the submarine, extricate himself with miraculous dexterity from the seemingly hopeless predicament in which we had left him the week before, only to become entangled in an even more desperate confrontation with death as the new chapter came to a close. We were hooked, of course, for the next adventure. In spite of my friendship with Tom and Dearie, I was never able to elicit a single clue on the outcome of the next episode. This may have been due to the lack of scripts, necessitating improvisation of most of the action as it was filmed. The American Film Company failed in 1918, the studio was sold, and the actors moved south to the new film Mecca, Hollywood.

* * *

In 1914 I attended a garden party with my parents at the home of the writer, Stewart Edward White. He had just returned from Africa and had filled a large studio at the rear of the garden with trophies of his safaris, which were still rarities at that time. This was my first confrontation with an author. Although too young to appreciate his talent, I was delighted by White's verbal account of his adventures in what seemed to me was the still dark and mysterious continent of Africa. White wrote, among other things, a novel of the American fur trade, *The Saga of Andy Burnett*, a subject which greatly interested me in later years.

My father shared many interests with Steward Edward White, including frequent target practice in Rattlesnake Canyon just back of town. Unfortunately, White moved to Burlingame after the First World War and gradually lost touch with my family. His former home on Los Olivos Street is now a nunnery.

* * *

In 1914 our fair city was blessed by the arrival of the second airplane. The first one had been piloted by Dadier Masson in 1911, but I was too young to remember that historic flight. The second flight was better publicized and created much more excitement. A special train ran some five miles to Hope Ranch where the plane was scheduled to take off. The fare was a quarter, and the train was jammed with enthusiasts, including my family. Everybody in town who could possibly get to Hope Ranch came to this gala event.

The airplane was piloted by a dare-devil stunt flier, Lincoln Beachey, who had become famous for looping the loop. His machine was a biplane that had been constructed in Los Angeles under the supervision of Glen Martin. It cost $10,000 and was powered by a $5,000 revolving-type engine of French design.

Beachey took off from a polo field and circled over Hope Ranch a couple of times at 2,000 feet. On the second turn he made a short dive and then looped the loop. As a result of this maneuver he lost control and began a series of gyrations which the crowd mistook for stunt flying. Finally he went into a side slip and, swinging around, pancaked on top of an oak tree close to where I was standing. I have a vivid recollection of an excited mob stampeding around the tree while the gallant aviator sat in the cockpit with his cap on backwards, nursing a bloody nose, and swearing like the trooper that he was. The crash was not serious, but a year later Lincoln Beachey, one of the truly great pioneers of flight, perished in another crash in San Francisco Bay.

Before Beachey's plane was wrecked in Hope Ranch it was used in a movie by the American Film Company. I'm indebted to John K. Northrup, who retired in Hope Ranch many years later, for this information, His father, Charles W. Northrup, was a contractor who added six feet to our dining room in 1916.

His son, a brilliant self-educated designer and engineer, worked in Santa Barbara from 1916 until 1920 for the Lockheed brothers, who had started the Lockheed Aircraft Corporation in a garage near the waterfront. He then left Santa Barbara to work for Donald Douglas and later founded his own company, the Northrop Corporation.

Allan and Malcolm Lockheed were enterprising young men who early entered the aviation field by building the Model G hydroplane in San Francisco in 1913 which flew 60 mph. It was used for passenger service during the Panama-Pacific Exposition and was later brought to Santa Barbara. My father went up in the Model G on January 6th, 1917. He also watched the construction of the world's largest hydroplane, the twin-engine F-1 on which John K. Northrup contributed his many talents.

In the summer of 1918 the F-1 was remodeled into a land plane for use on a promotional transcontinental flight to Washington, D.C. Unfortunately it was grounded in Arizona due to engine trouble. It was returned to Santa Barbara, reconverted to a flying boat in 1919, and used for sightseeing. Allan was the pilot, Malcolm was the co-pilot, and there were additional seats for eight passengers. Mary Miles Minter was credited with being the first guest to fly in this plane, and the King and Queen of Belgium were up that summer for a memorable view of Santa Barbara.

On July 9th my brother Dick and I went for our first plane ride but on separate flights. The F-1 taxied across the harbor, finally attaining an altitude of several hundred feet. We flew south for six miles, circling the

Miramar Hotel, and returned to Santa Barbara. It was an exciting, noisy ride, and the vibrations in the open cockpit were rather frightening to an eleven-year-old boy. My mother was indignant when she heard of our flights and forbade us to have anything further to do with airplanes.

* * *

As a youngster I took special delight in the older people who came to our house. They were nearly always good story-tellers and enthralled me with tales of high adventure which I longed to emulate. There were many fascinating personalities living right in our neighborhood. One of them was Charles A. Storke, a printer who came to Santa Barbara in 1872 and homesteaded one hundred and twenty-three acres on a hill back of town, which is now the fashionable Riviera. Storke had enlisted in the Thirty-Sixth Wisconsin Volunteers during the Civil War at the age of sixteen and was one of only twelve survivors in his regiment after the Battle of the Wilderness. He was captured June 1st, 1864, and was sent to Andersonville, Libby, and other prisons. Due to his youth he was paroled on December 13th, 1864. Later he became the first student to enroll at Cornell. He was fond of walking near our home, and I longed to ask him why he hadn't tunnelled out of those hellholes as I imagined I could have done, but he was so dour of countenance that I dared not ask. Actually, the terrible ordeal of three months affected him for the rest of his life.

His son, Thomas M. Storke, owned a local newspaper and years later won a Pulitzer Prize for his brilliant editorials against the John Birch Society. He had a son named Charley, and one day after school I became involved in a mudball and lemon fight in the Storkes' back yard on Santa Barbara Street. When Tom Storke came home and saw the devastation in his garden, for which I was largely responsible, he warned Charley that I was a juvenile delinquent with definite criminal tendencies and predicted that I would end up in San Quentin prison.

Three weeks later I was arrested with two other boys for holding onto a streetcar while riding our bicycles. While we were waiting in the police court along with other petty criminals, T. M. Storke walked in to see the judge. I have never forgotten the smug, triumphant expression on his face which seemed to say, "there goes that young rascal on his first step toward San Quentin." I reminded Mr. Storke of his dire prediction when he was ninety-two and assured him that there was still time for his prophecy to be fulfilled.

Thomas M. Storke had sized up my character correctly, for my criminal tendencies soon progressed to dynamiting. On a train returning from San Francisco I stole a dynamite cap from a canister hanging on the observation platform. These powerful explosives were placed on railroad tracks by conductors to signal on-coming trains before electric devices were installed.

I placed the stolen cap on the streetcar track on Garden Street opposite Alameda Park and hid behind a hedge with a group of schoolboys to await results. Soon a trolley came rattling along full of old ladies returning from shopping downtown. The explosion was more thunderous than we had expected and seemed to lift the front of the car several inches off the tracks. The conductor and his terrified passengers filed out in utter confusion, while we rolled on the grass, convulsed with laughter. Fortunately no harm was done, nor were we apprehended.

* * *

Half a block north on Laguna Street was the home of the Lockwood de Forests. They had gone to India in 1880, and Mrs. de Forest claimed to be the first white woman to visit Nepal, having been carried over the mountain pass in a palanquin. Happily endowed with independent means (Mrs. de Forest's mother was a duPont) they spent a number of years collecting Indian artifacts, not only for themselves, but for several museums. They were especially interested in the elaborate teak carvings of Lahore, stone grills, and the beautiful cotton materials used by Indian women for saris. De Forest was a talented landscape painter, and his brother, Robert, was for many years President of the Board of Trustees of the Metropolitan Museum in New York.

My interest in art began in their large house—a veritable wonderland of Oriental splendor filled with Indian handicrafts of superlative workmanship; Damascus chests inlaid with ivory and mother-of-pearl; Damascus tiles, cottons, brocades; Benares brass trays; and a fabulous collection of Indian jewelry.

Curious obsessions often afflict the aged and so it was with Lockwood de Forest, whose chief worry was a tall eucalyptus tree that grew a few inches beyond our property line. He had grown so deaf that communication with him was virtually impossible and he had developed a loud and continuous hum. Once a month he would appear in our back yard, circling the tree, humming in anger as he went, and making gestures of cutting it down. I was usually sent to placate the old man and would shout in vain that even if he wanted to it wasn't ours to saw down. This symbolic ritual of decapitation would appease his wrath, and he'd hum his way only to reappear a month later.

THE COURTHOUSE

On the walls around Napoleon are depicted
His true remains. These studied images,
Civic narrations and expectancies,
Move those who go to wonder at his tomb
Like shapes that move through water as a wave.

Our Moorish-Latin courthouse! Murals bring
Cabrillo shoreward, Junipero Serra's flock
Watch blind desire apportion earth and sea
On scales of gold. Green tree and kingly ranch
Spread from imperial oil to the western gate.

Acres of flowers for seed; nearby, dry fields
For blast-off, for failure and failed ambition
Past intimate horizon to the far.
We who had sought the symbols of the spirit
To have life more abundantly, discoverers

From spirit's old anxiety, explore
The courtrooms like a logic, for a premise,
Uneasy before the flags and photographs
Of boys who traveled east to fight a war
With other boys equally free and brave.

Edgar Bowers
— 1989

J. Smeaton Chase (1864-1923) came to California in 1890 from his native England. He traveled throughout the state, writing a half-dozen books about its natural wonders. His finest book, California Coast Trails *(1913), is a narrative of the 1911 horseback trip up the coast. It contains a glimpse of Santa Barbara.*

SANTA BARBARA TRAILS

THE NAME OF THIS village [Carpinteria] offers an example of the manner in which a great number of places in the State came by their titles. This and many other points on the coast were named by members of the expedition (of which Father Palou was the historian) which passed up the coast by land from San Diego to Monterey in the year 1769. At this spot some Indians were found engaged in building a canoe, and from that circumstance the soldiers of the party named the place by the Spanish word for carpenter's shop. Similarly, from nothing more important than the killing of a gull, a point a few miles to the west was named Gaviota. That the clergy also took their full share in the work of bestowing titles is plain enough from the generous manner in which the saints were remembered.

I had heard of a celebrated grapevine hereabouts which proclaims itself the Goliath of its kind. I turned aside to see it, and found the monster in an enclosure behind a little house which stands on the site of a vanished adobe. When I viewed the enormous trunk, nearly ten feet in girth, I could easily credit its claim as to size, and the statement of its owner that it bore from six to twelve tons of fruit yearly. The limbs (one of which I measured and found it three and a half feet around) cover a space a hundred feet square, and are supported on a framework of massive timbers. There is a legend that it dates from the year 1809, the birth year of so many great men; but be that as it may, it shows no sign of decay, and should be good for many a decade, in proof of one "tall California story," at least. I bought a bottle of juice made from its grapes, and ate my lunch under the ample shade, looking, I was aware, like a sort of modern and commonplace Silenus.

From the increasing number of automobiles that bequeathed us their superfluous dust and odors, I knew that we were nearing Santa Barbara. We were, in fact, already within the limits of the generous grant of lands which belonged of old to the Spanish *pueblo*. A few miles brought us to Summerland, where a number of black and oily derricks built on wharves are robbing Neptune of a long unsuspected asset. The place, which was originally a Spiritualist colony, now resounds with the creak and groan of pumping-plants, and at night might, I should think, still be a congenial rendezvous for ghosts.

On the right now appeared the wooded slopes of Montecito, a lovely expanse of rolling country sacred to millionaires. A green canyon of oaks and sycamores suggested thoughts of camping, but there was something almost sacrilegious in the idea, and I hastened on. Oak-shaded villas gave place to acres of sweet-pears and trim orchards of walnut and orange, and beyond ran the dreamy blue mountains with the peak of La Cumbre overlooking all. Soon the dust of the road was exchanged for asphalt, and gay parties of Barbareños appeared in automobiles and on horseback in quest of appetites for dinner. By early evening I rode into Santa Barbara, and for a day or two we went into city quarters.

When, in 1835, Dana sailed into Santa Barbara Bay on the Pilgrim, he found (to quote his own words) "the large bay without a vessel in it; the surf roaring and rolling in upon the beach; the white Mission, the dark town, and the high, treeless mountains." The three quarters of a century that has elapsed since that time has been highly eventful to California as a whole, but as usual the caprices of fortune have had their effect. Santa Barbara then, notwithstanding the poor impression Dana received of it, was the place of second importance in the Californias, outranked only by

Monterey, the capital. San Francisco was a "newly begun settlement, mostly of Yankee Californians, called Yerba Buena, which promises well"; and Los Angeles, though then the largest town in California, could hardly have dreamed, with her interior position, of contending for the southern supremacy with the better placed settlements on the coast.

The modern city of Santa Barbara is a place of about twelve thousand people, which, wisely following the lines of least resistance, has attained a fame of its own as a particularly delightful place of residence. Its climate, mild, equable, and the reverse of stimulating, is just suited to the enjoyment of its attractions of coast and mountain scenery; and tourists, who nowadays "with extensive View, survey Mankind from China to Peru," naturally have not overlooked Santa Barbara. Two giant hotels provide the superlative of comfort for the wealthy traveller, and streets of pretty houses in flower-crammed gardens are inhabited by fugitives from blizzard-stricken States in East and North.

There are not many traces, except in the names of several of the streets, of the older Santa Barbara. Of what remains of it the Mission stands first in interest. It dates from 1786, and, standing on the high ground at the rear of the city, the gray old building, drowsing in the sun, with its red-tiled corridors and twin domed belfries, sheds an air of Spanish languor, of perpetual siesta, over the city.

While I sat on the bench beside the fountain in the open space before the Mission, I heard the patter of naked feet beside me, and, turning, saw the arch face of a Mexican boy of seven or eight years only a few paces away. He had noticed my camera, and was skirmishing in hope of some interesting photographic incident, but was ready for flight at a moment's notice. When I spoke to him he came and talked frankly, telling me his name, José, and those of his father and a considerable array of brothers and sisters. The surname was that of one of the soldiers who formed the escort of Padre Lasuen at the time of the founding of the Mission, and as it was an unusual name I had little doubt that this curly-pated youngster was one link of a chain which, if I could trace it, would lead back to that event—one of some importance in the history of the State.

69

The Mission possesses a great collection of the material of California history, On the library of the building I found the genial and scholarly Father Zephyrin Engelhardt, deep in learned labors over his great "History of the Franciscan Missions," now issuing from the press. It is a worthy task, and Protestants as well as Catholics may well regard with respect the work of Father Serra and his helpers on these shores, which, a century and quarter ago, were more remote and savage than Central Africa is today.

On a quiet side street I found another remnant of Santa Barbara's historic past—the old mansion of the de la Guerras, a family so identified with the city that its history might almost be said to be their own. Readers may remember that it is the marriage of one of the daughters of this house, Doña Anita de la Guerra de Noriega y Carrillo, that Dana describes with so much vivacity. The bridegroom was Mr. Alfred Robinson, the agent of the owners of the Pilgrim and the Alert. (There is a volume, now rare, entitled "Life in California, by an American," written by this Mr. Robinson, which gives much very interesting information as to manners and affairs in California a decade or two before the grand transition from hides and tallow to gold.)

I noticed over the main doorway of the house the words, in quaint lettering, "La paz sea en esta casa" (Peace be to this house), followed by the name of the family. There seemed an odd disparity between the sentiment and the martial name (for de la Guerra signifies, literally, "of the war"). I wondered whether the incongruity could have been unnoticed by the old don who had the words cut there, or whether there may not have been some particular occasion for the little joke.

I believe it has been found that the western coast of this continent is slowly rising. If that be so, and the movement is to go on, and no wholly unthinkable change is to arise in the course of human affairs, why, I wondered, may not this sleepy city be a far future metropolis of the Western Hemisphere, lying at the head of a huge bay protected by a great arm of land on which the present Channel Islands would be prominent peaks? But no doubt, long before that could come to pass, ports,

70

steamships, and all the rest of our modern paraphernalia will be matter of very ancient history; and meanwhile Santa Barbara fulfills her comfortable destiny, dozing among palms and roses beside the blues of seas.

PERSIMMON HILL, SANTA BARBARA '78

Sorrowful months of
unusual rain stunt fluffy asters sowed
under last cool March's invisible moon.
On the underground radio broken
voices report uncovered mass graves of
proud Huehuetenango's slaughtered
children.

Spittle bug suck at delicate
stems of dainty wallflowers companion
planted with hoped for pearly tuberoses.
Streamside our flower field common
crow watch us plant Aztec zinnias just
before the red Toltec sun comes down.
The Taliking windbreak eucalyptus an-
nounces scattered radioactive air from
innocently spilt over stainless steel can-
nisters in transit through the nearby
Mediterranean style adobe airport.

I wander down rows of
baby's breath avoiding husks of dead
caterpillars. Yesterday spread the last
volunteer ranunculus on R.'s still un-
marked grave. Just Christmas before last
his breath too withered to read his own
poems.

Paul Portugés
—1984

Stewart Edward White (1873-1946) was one of the most popular American writers of his day, probably Santa Barbara's first modern celebrity. He wrote of the boom years of the 1880s in his novel, The Rose Dawn *(1920) and gave a non-fiction portrait of the Santa Barbara back country in* The Mountains *(1904).*

THE RIDGE TRAIL

SIX TRAILS LEAD TO THE MAIN RIDGE. They are all good trails, so that even the casual tourist in the little Spanish-American town on the seacoast need have nothing to fear from the ascent. In some spots they contract to an arm's length of space, outside of which limit they drop sheer away; elsewhere they stand up on end, zigzag in lacets each more hair-raising than the last, or fill to demoralization with loose boulders and shale. A fall on the part of your horse would mean a more than serious accident; but Western horses do not fall. The major premise stands: even the casual tourist has no real reason for fear, however scared he may become.

Our favorite route to the main ridge was by a way called the Cold Spring Trail. We used to enjoy taking visitors up it, mainly because you come on the top suddenly, without warning. Then we collected remarks. Everybody, even the most stolid, said something.

You rode three miles on the flat, two in the leafy and gradually ascending creek-bed of a canyon, a half hour of laboring steepness in the overarching mountain lilac and laurel. There you came to a great rock gateway which seemed the top of the world. At the gateway was a Bad Place where the ponies planted warily their little hoofs, and the visitor played "eyes front," and besought that his mount should not stumble.

Beyond the gateway a lush level canyon into which you plunged as into a bath; then again the laboring trail, up and always up toward the blue California sky, out of the lilacs, and laurels, and redwood chaparral into the manzanita, the Spanish bayonet, the creamy yucca, and the fine angular shale of the upper regions. Beyond the apparent summit you found always other summits yet to be climbed. And all at once, like thrusting your shoulders out of a hatchway, you looked over the top.

Then came the remarks. Some swore softly; some uttered appreciative ejaculation; some shouted aloud; some gasped; one man uttered three times the word "Oh,"—once breathlessly, Oh! once in awakening appreciation, Oh! once in wild enthusiasm, OH! Then invariably they fell silent and looked.

For the ridge, ascending from seaward in a gradual coquetry of foothills, broad low ranges, cross-systems, canyons, little flats, and gentle ravines inland dropped off almost sheer to the river below. And from under your feet rose, range after range, tier after tier, rank after rank, in increasing crescendo of wonderful tinted mountains to the main crest of the Coast Ranges, the blue distance, the mightiness of California's western systems. The eye followed them up and up, and farther and farther, with the accumulating emotion of a wild rush on a toboggan. There came a point where the fact grew to be almost too big for the appreciation, just as beyond a certain point speed seems to become unbearable. It left you breathless, wonder-stricken, awed. You could do nothing but look, and look, and look again, tongue-tied by the impossibility of doing justice to what you felt. And in the far distance, finally, your soul, grown big in a moment, came to rest on the great precipices and pines of the greatest mountains of all, close under the sky.

In a little, after the change has come to you, a change definite and enduring, which left your inner processes forever different from what they had been, you turned sharp to the west and rode five miles along the knife-edge Ridge Trail to where Rattlesnake Canyon led you down and back to your accustomed environment.

To the left as you rode you saw, far on the horizon, rising to the height of your eye, the mountains of the Channel Islands. Then the deep sapphire of the Pacific, fringed with the soft, unchanging white of the surf and the yellow of the shore. Then the town like a little map, and the lush greens of the wide meadows, the fruit-groves, the lesser ranges—all vivid, fertile, brilliant, and pulsating with vitality. You filled your senses with it, steeped them in the beauty of it. And at once, by a mere turn of the eyes, from the almost crude insistence of the bright primary color of life, you faced the tenuous azures of distance, the delicate mauves and amethysts, the lilacs and saffrons of the arid country.

This was the wonder we never tired of seeing for ourselves, of showing to others. And often, academically, perhaps a little wistfully, as one talks of something to be dreamed of but never enjoyed, we spoke of how fine it would be to ride down into that land of mystery and enchantment, to penetrate one after another the canyons dimly outlined in the shadows cast by the westering sun, to cross the mountains lying outspread in easy grasp of the eye, to gain the distant blue Ridge, and see with our own eyes what lay beyond.

For to its other attractions the prospect added that of impossibility, of unattainableness. These rides of ours were day rides. We had to get home by nightfall. Our horses had to be fed, ourselves to be housed. We had not time to continue on down the other side whither the trail led. At the very and literal brink of achievement we were forced to turn back.

Gradually the idea possessed us. We promised ourselves that some day we would explore. In our after-dinner smokes we spoke of it. Occasionally, from some hunter or forest ranger, we gained little items of information, we learned the fascination of musical names—Mono Canyon, Patrera Don Victor, Lloma Paloma, Patrera Madulce, Cuyamas, became familiar to us as syllables. We desired mightily to body them forth to ourselves as facts. The extent of our mental vision expanded. We heard of other mountains far beyond these farthest—mountains whose almost unexplored vastnesses contained great forests, mighty valleys, strong water-courses, beautiful hanging-meadows, deep canyons of granite, eternal snows,—mountains so extended, so wonderful, that their secrets offered whole summers of solitary exploration. We came to feel their marvel, we came to respect the inferno of the Desert that hemmed them in. Shortly we graduated from the indefiniteness of railroad maps to the intricacies of geological survey charts. The fever was on us. We must go.

    A dozen of us desired. Three of us went; and of the manner of our going, and what you must know who would do likewise, I shall try here to tell.

NADA MAS
for T. Clark

A seasalty breeze carries up the hill
to our aviary of sunsplattered green,
where a siamese cat named Purgato
tightropes a bleached wooden fence
stalking scent of neon fish
beneath stray somersaulting clouds.
A turkey vulture circles
in a sky now cellophane white,
as day inflates like a balloon
with interiors emptied out
past the speed of light,
another missile-range miscue?
I drink a glass of bottled water,
watch smoldering verdant chrome.

David Dahl
—1984

ROBERT HYDE

Bobby Hyde (1900-1969) is remembered as the father of Santa Barbara Bohemia, the creator of the Mountain Drive subculture of the 1950s and 60s. His most popular book was Six More at Sixty *(1960), a story of affectionate incidents and local color about the adoption of the six Rodriguez children by Hyde and his wife Floppy.*

SIX MORE AT SIXTY

 IN A LIFETIME OF WRITING, the best work I have ever done was forty years ago at the age of 19, without either experience or information, inventing fairy tales about the Gobi Desert, a place few people have ever been, certainly not myself. Since then there have been the obstructing considerations which stand in the way of all writers. Every good story is scandalous and true, one you don't dare write because some reader would recognize the characters in it even if you changed the names and altered the details until you had ruined the story. Otherwise it is one you invented out of the purest air according to the magazine formula, all about attractive young people with a problem of the heart or pocketbook, and nobody believes a word of such pipe dreams. Acceptable writing has to steer a tight course between one more Scylla and Charybdis: if you make the manuscript too interesting, it will be banned; too innocuous, it will not sell.

In comparison with what my contemporaries have dared, my work has suffered from innocuousness. That would account for such small, valuable editions and such an elite, exclusive public. But I have never before had a message to deliver!

Here is a message so important that in spite of the millions of words of practice (unconsciously in training for this moment) I don't know how to start. Looking over my shoulder are the wide, anxious eyes in too many wistful faces. The little ghosts watch with bated breath, urging me on, hoping that in spite of all inadequacies I will, through some miracle, speak for them. Scattered all over the world are children without parents, parents without children . . .

Many of those children must be as wonderful as ours. It is hard to believe, but mathematics makes it so. It would be too much of a coincidence if our children were extraordinary. And many lonely adults would be better parents than we are.

Now that our children have lived here five years it becomes next to impossible to think back to that morning when we stood out in the bright sunlight in the turnaround as Faith Tuck drove up in her car.

Afterwards Ruthie would tell us how we looked that morning through their eyes. "I was almost sick to my stomach when I got here. I always got sick when I rode in a car. You and Mommy looked so funny! You and Mommy were laughing so hard!"

We reached through the window of Faith's car and hugged the six of them and kissed them. They spilled out onto the ground and began scurrying about like rabbits. In no time they were sweeping the withered olive leaves out of the empty swimming pool so they could put water in it. Then they dropped the brooms and paraded shyly through the house, touching each piece of furniture as they passed, getting used to the idea that this was where they were going to live, slowly possessing it.

"What shall we call you?" they wanted to know at last.

Floppy said, "He's Bobby and I'm Floppy."

"Floppy!" Becky shrieked.

They couldn't believe anybody was really called Floppy.

There were plenty of children who called their parents by a first name, but it had always seemed affected to me. I wanted this family to be as normal as possible. They ought to call us Mommy and Daddy. I told them so.

They were embarrassed at first. If one of them called me anything but Daddy I said, "I don't know you." They thought that was pretty funny, but they found out I meant it. To get cooperation out of me they had to call me Daddy. They all capitulated but Martha. She persisted in calling us Bobby and Floppy. She decided to be our contemporary, not our child. Martha refused to adopt us.

* * *

We live on a brushy slope of the coast range—with the air clean and warm, little traffic, houses several hundred feet apart—good country for children to grow up in. Of course there is poison oak in the canyons and occasionally a scorpion on the floor. In the fall the tarantulas cross Coyote Road toward higher ground. It is the first warning of the rains to come. Time to get up on the roof and patch the leaks when you see tarantulas on the march. When a child appears at breakfast with a big welt on his face or arms he has probably been host during the night to a western blood-sucking conenose. Conenoses breed in pack-rat nests. Farther south, if the rat is infected, the conenose may carry the fearful Chagas disease. Once or twice a year somebody kills a snake. Little boys treasure the rattles and gourmets digest the steaks. There's a vigorous earthquake once every generation or so. And the mountains burn off periodically as they have since the beginning of time. There was lightning to ignite the brush long before cancer addicts flipped butts into the dry grass. But every locality has its drawbacks, and we prefer the drawbacks of ours.

If we didn't like our neighbors we would have nobody but ourselves to blame, because we chose them. When moved into this spot we were here alone. The forty or more families now living around us bought land either from us or from our friends or children.

Only one neighbor bridled when the Rodriguezes came to live with us. A southerner who lives in a trailer with her own large family of children while she builds her adobe house said, "Robert, you certainly don't intend to keep them!"

"We certainly do," I said. To balance that tentative objection there were open arms everywhere. There is no segregation here. Two Negro families who intended to buy here changed their plans to our regret. We have had Negro tenants. We have offered land to Chinese, Hindus, Japanese, and Filipinos, and a family of Spanish Californians is buying land at the moment.

In most cases our neighbors are people who were glad to move onto their acre for fifty dollars down and fifty dollars a month and never have to pay rent again. There are seventy-five children in those forty homemade houses.

Since we have two families of our own grandchildren living within visiting distance, some voice might well demand, "What are you two doing with foster children? Why don't you resign yourselves gracefully to being grandparents?"

Having grandchildren who live with their own mothers and fathers doesn't fill the bill if you want children under your own roof. The time you spend with children is the fringe time, before school, after school, at supper, between music lessons and playtime and at bedtime. You love your grandchildren and you see them regularly but they live in their family by the rules of their family. If you feel the temptation to influence your grandchildren, you are wise to resist it. You think twice before correcting your son-in-law's or daughter-in-law's children. The fact of relationship gives grandparents not more privilege but less, and you would be more influential as a stranger. Not that you simply have to influence somebody—but when you love children you want their faults corrected.

A few years ago in our kitchen an occasional avocado seed would be scooped out of its expensive, pistachio-green hollow to make place for a spoonful of french dressing. The seeds were fat and vital and we planted them first in buttermilk cartons in leaf mold and then on the slope south of the house. Now the trees from those seeds are bearing fruit you have to reach from the top of a ladder.

Step ladders aren't made for side hills, so I hold the ladder while a child climbs it, breaks the fruit off, and hands it down. Some fruit can be reached by climbing the trees themselves, but most of it dangles out of reach at the ends of branches. For my birthday the children gave me an avocado picker with a long aluminum handle, remote control clippers, and a little canvas sack. It gets used every day, year in, year out.

The skirts of avocado trees sweep the hillside, some of the fruit lying on the ground like melons. When the crop begins to ripen we pick those first so gophers, pack rats, and possums won't get them before we do. We have only our engrafted seedlings, each with its independent season, its different fruit. For a money crop seedlings would be hopeless, but for feeding our Rodriguezes, what could be better?

Avocados were an important part of our menu even when we had to buy them. They supply vegetable oils difficult to come by in any other way. We planted those seeds for our Rodriguezes, but we didn't know it then. Ixtapetl must have worked on us by remote control.

We planted guava seeds, too, and citrus, pomegranates, and grapes. Seeds are to plant. There is a long-standing cooperation between men and plants, and whosoever enjoys the fruit should plant the seed. Practiced as a rite of thanks, it is not so irksome as the same operation for a motive of gain. The bioethic is signed in sap and plasma. We trifle with it at our peril.

Seedlings from the guavas and avocados we ate five years ago are feeding us lavishly today. Grafting is a wonderful device of course, but it stands as a bugaboo between most people and the seedling orchards they could have with little effort or cost. Our Rodriguezes are demonstrating the health that comes with fruit ripened on the tree in the yard. Our real harvest is their health.

Pomegranates that weigh a pound grow on our seedlings. Sapotes, cherimoyas, macadamia nuts, passion fruit, loquats, and apricots are coming along. We have picked two pineapples from plants we grew by rooting the discarded tops, and we're not green thumbs either.

The gophers are always after our trees, so instead of trapping them we plant everything in wire baskets, then let the gophers do our weeding and mulching for us. That makes it easier on us and on the gophers, too.

Our biggest crop is olives, but the hand labor limits it. Twenty ancient trees grow around the house. As young trees, nearly a century ago, they came from Italy to a big ranch south of here. Fifteen years ago, when olives in the valley were being bulldozed to make place for lemons, we salvaged our trees with a winch truck and rolled them into hastily dug holes on our barren hilltop. Water had to be hauled in barrels until I had time to dig a well in the canyon and lay eight hundred feet of pipe, install a pump, and string wire to pump water up the hill.

We harvest olives for pickling while the fruit is still rosy, straw-colored or green. I try to pick from the step ladder and leave lower branches so the children can pick them from the ground or by standing on chairs.

Becky demands, "Let me on the ladder, Daddy!"

I point to the branches near the ground. "I can't reach that low. I'd have to lie on my stomach."

"But I want to be on the ladder, Daddy!"

While I empty the carton Becky pre-empts the ladder.

"Let me pick on the ladder, Daddy, you have to—you let Becky!"

They take over the ladder and I stand on the chair.

Crocks of brightly colored olives look like hoards of jewels in Aladdin's cave. We stand the fruit in lye solution overnight, pour off the lye, and wash for five days. Then the olives go in light brine and we can eat them. Still all colors, they shine like jewels and the children gobble them and smack their lips. Home-cured olives must be eaten soon, not left to culture botulinus.

When we harvest for olive oil it doesn't matter if the fruit is bruised. The children enjoy that harvest the best. Even neighbor children gather for the fun of lashing the trees with bamboo sticks and feeling the fruit pelt down on them like hail. Everywhere little figures scamper about with boxes, climb ladders, whack the trees with poles, lift the edges of plastic sheets to herd the black marbles into central piles. Other harvesters squat on the ground scavenging fruit whacked too far or knocked down by birds. If we get a good wind at olive-picking time we stand in the full force of it and pour olives from one pail to another. The leaves and twigs blow away, leaving the olives ready to grind and press.

At every stage of the gathering, crushing, and pressing rises the pungent inviting smell of olives, a constant assurance that we are satisfying a basic hunger.

We shred the olives in the meat grinder, press the pulp in strong sacks with an automobile jack. The light oil rises at once in the juice and lies sweet and golden on top of the bitter olive wine. The oil is ready to eat and can go straight into a salad. Or into a bowl with pickled olives and a crushed clove of garlic!

Few people have tasted the flavor of fresh olive oil, so sweet, delicate, and clean you can drink it. But if sunlight touches any part of the process the true flavor is lost. Like butter, olive oil cannot endure sunlight.

Harvesting of the olive crop has to pay off in its own subtle satisfactions. It doesn't make sense any other way. The Japanese say that pleasure is not in the objective, but in the many pleasant steps by which the objective is attained. Picking olives puts you at peace with yourself. You can suddenly think more clearly about a thousand things which have no relation to olives. When I get to be an old man no use for anything else, there will still be olives to pick. It's good to have a project ready.

✳ ✳ ✳

Helen Pedotti wanted some olive trees for her garden, so Lloyd and I dug out two of the several hundred at Maria Ygnacia, trucked them to her town house, and planted them. Olive trees like to travel. We have transplanted dozens from our canyon, but the ones that are left quickly branch out and fill the space.

If you haven't a steady job in this town, you make a living any way you can. We used to cut firewood with a buzz saw and deliver and stack it. We used to crawl on our hands and knees under the chaparral in the canyons, collecting leaf mold we could sell for a dollar a sack at the farmers' market. I have built brick and stone fireplaces and stone walls and a dozen or more houses. Stokowski hired me to build his house for him. It took several years and supported us during the depression.

"Teach me to build a house," said Stoky. "I'll teach you to conduct an orchestra!"

From AT LOS OLIVOS AND ALAMEDA PADRE SERRA

Below St. Mary's retreat
In its greenery, on its hill
Are some unowned olive trees
Backed by a stone wall
in a crook of the busy street.
You can visit them when you please.

Though trucks gear down and brake,
Growling and hissing, and cars
Whoosh by the place all day,
The light's clear there, the gray
Grove whitens, when it stirs,
As if for its own sake.

The ground is packed and bare
And stained bright purple and black
From the unpicked bitter fruit
That spurt from underfoot,
Walking, I do not lack
For quiet in that air.

*

Winter dusk, and I peer
From the stone bridge nearby
Through alder and sycamore
At the stream racing high
And red with mountain mud
And listen till I hear
Under the water-roar
The streambed boulders thud
And see them gone dead white
And silent at this spot,
And the last pool sunk from sight,
And the clear, weightless current
Of the air quivering hot
Over the solid torrent.

Alan Stephens
— 1982

84

Kenneth Millar (1915-1983) wrote his detective novels under the name Ross Macdonald. Undoubtedly the most important literary presence in post-War Santa Barbara, many of his stories are set in the Santa Barbara facsimile, "Santa Teresa" and play off real events such as the 1964 Coyote fire, as did The Underground Man (1971).

THE UNDERGROUND MAN

I

 BEFORE WE REACHED SANTA TERESA I could smell smoke. Then I could see it dragging like a veil across the face of the mountain behind the city.

Under and through the smoke I caught glimpses of fire like the flashes of heavy guns too far away to be heard. The illusion of war was completed by an old two-engine bomber which flew in low over the mountain's shoulder. The plane was lost in the smoke for a long instant, then climbed out trailing a pastel red cloud of fire retardant.

On the freeway ahead the traffic thickened rapidly and stopped us. I reached over to turn on the car radio but then decided not to. The woman beside me had enough on her mind without having to listen to fire reports.

At the head of the line, a highway patrolman was directing the movement of traffic from a side road onto the freeway. There were quite a few cars coming down out of the hills, many of them with Santa Teresa college decals. I noticed several trucks piled with furniture and mattresses, children and dogs.

When the patrolman let us pass, we turned onto the road that led to the hills. It took us in a gradual climb between lemon groves and subdivisions toward what Jean described as Mrs. Broadhurst's canyon.

A man wearing a Forest Service jacket and a yellow hard hat stopped the Mercedes at the entrance to the canyon. Jean climbed out and introduced herself as Mrs. Broadhurst's daughter-in-law.

"I hope you're not planning to stay, ma'am. We may have to evacuate this area."

"Have you seen my husband and little boy?" She described Ronny—six years old, blue eyes, black-haired, wearing a light-blue suit.

He shook his head. "I've seen a lot of people leaving with their kids. It isn't a bad idea. Once the fire starts spilling down one of these canyons she can outrace you."

"How bad is it?" I said.

"It depends on the wind. If the wind stays quiet we could get her fully contained before nightfall. We've got a lot of equipment up on the mountain. But if she starts to blow—" He lifted his hand in a kind of resigned goodbye to everything in sight.

We drove into the canyon between fieldstone gate posts emblazoned with the name Canyon Estates. New and expensive houses were scattered along the canyonside among the oaks and boulders. Men and women with hoses were watering their yards and buildings and the surrounding brush. Their children were watching them, or sitting quietly in cars, ready to go. The smoke towering up from the mountain stood over them like a threat and changed the color of the light.

The Broadhurst ranch lay between these houses and the fire. We went up the canyon toward it, and left the county road at Mrs. Broadhurst's mailbox. Her private asphalt lane wound through acres of mature avocado trees. Their broad leaves were shriveling at the tips as if the fire had already touched them. Darkening fruit hung down from their branches like green hand grenades.

The lane broadened into a circular drive in front of a large and simple white stucco ranchhouse. Under the deep porch, red fuchsias dripped from hanging redwood baskets. At a red glass hummingbird feeder suspended among the baskets, a hummingbird which also seemed suspended was sipping from a spout and treading air.

The bird didn't move perceptibly when a woman opened the screen door and came out. She had on a white shirt and dark slacks which showed off her narrow waist. She moved across the veranda with rapid disciplined energy, making the high heels of her riding boots click.

"Jean darling."

"Mother."

They shook hands briefly like competitors before a match of some kind. Mrs. Broadhurst's neat dark head was touched with gray, but she was younger than I'd imagined, no more than fifty or so.

Only her eyes looked older. Without moving them from Jean's face, she shook her head from side to side.

"No, they haven't come back. And they haven't been seen in the area for some time. Who's the blond girl?"

"I don't know."

"Is Stanley having an affair with her?"

"I don't know, Mother." She turned to me. "This is Mr. Archer."

Mrs. Broadhurst nodded curtly. "Jean mentioned on the telephone that you're some kind of detective. Is that correct?"

"The private kind."

She raked me with a look that moved from my eyes down to my shoes and back up to my face again. "I've never set much store in private detectives, frankly. But under the circumstances perhaps you can be useful. If the radio can be believed, the fire has passed the Mountain House and left it untouched. Would you like to come up there with me?"

"I would. After I talk to the gardener."

"That won't be necessary."

"But I understand he gave your son a key to the Mountain House. He may know why they wanted it."

"He doesn't. I've questioned Fritz. We're wasting time, and I've already wasted a good deal. I stayed by the telephone until you and Jean got here."

"Where is Fritz?"

"You're persistent, aren't you? He may be in the lath house."

We left Jean standing white-faced and apprehensive in the shadow of the veranda. The lath house was in a walled garden behind one wing of the ranchhouse. Mrs. Broadhurst followed me in under the striped shadows cast by the roof.

"Fritz? Mr. Archer wants to ask you a question."

A soft-looking man in dungarees straightened up from the plants he was tending. He had emotional green eyes and a skittish way of holding his body, as if he was ready to avoid a threatened blow. There was a livid scar connecting his mouth and his nose which looked as if he had been born with a harelip.

"What is it this time?" he said.

"I'm trying to find out what Stanley Broadhurst is up to. Why do you think he wanted the key to the guest house?"

Fritz shrugged his thick loose shoulders. "I don't know. I can't read people's minds, can I?"

"You must have some idea."

He glanced uncomfortably at Mrs. Broadhurst. "Am I supposed to spit it all out?"

"Please tell the truth," she said in a forced tone.

"Well, naturally I thought him and the chick had hanky-panky in mind. Why else would they want to go up there?"

"With my grandson along?" Mrs. Broadhurst said.

"They wanted me to keep the boy with me. But I didn't want the responsibility. That's the way you get in trouble," he said with stupid wisdom.

"You didn't mention that before. You should have told me, Fritz."

"I can't remember everything at once, can I?"

"How was the boy behaving?" I asked him.

"Okay. He didn't say much."

"Neither do you."

"What do you want me to say? You think I did something to the boy?" His voice rose, and his eyes grew moist and suddenly overflowed.

88

'Nobody suggested anything like that."

"Then why do you keep at me and at me? The boy was here with his father. His father took him away. Does that make me responsible?"

"Take it easy."

Mrs. Broadhurst touched my arm. "We're getting nowhere."

We left the gardener complaining among his plants. The striped shadow fell from the roof, jailbirding him.

The carport was attached to an old red barn at the back of the house. Below the barn was a dry creekbed at the bottom of a shallow ravine which was thickly grown with oaks and eucalyptus. Band-tailed pigeons and sweet-voiced red-winged blackbirds were foraging under the trees and around a feeder. I stepped on fallen eucalyptus pods which looked like ornate bronze nailheads set in the dust.

An aging Cadillac and an old pickup stood under the carport. Mrs. Broadhurst drove the pickup, wrestling it angrily around the curves in the avocado grove and turning left on the road toward the mountains. Beyond the avocados were ancient olive trees, and beyond them was pasture gone to brush.

We were approaching the head of the canyon. The smell of burning grew stronger in my nostrils. I felt as though we were going against nature, but I didn't mention my qualms to Mrs. Broadhurst. She wasn't the sort of woman you confessed human weakness to.

The road degenerated as we climbed. It was narrow and inset with boulders. Mrs. Broadhurst jerked at the wheel of the truck as if it was a male animal resisting control. For some reason I was reminded of Mrs. Roger Armistead's voice on the phone, and I asked Mrs. Broadhurst if she knew the woman.

She answered shortly: "I've seen her at the beach club. Why do you ask?"

"The Armistead name came up in connection with your son's friend, the blond girl."

"How?"

"She was using their Mercedes."

"I'm not surprised at the connection. The Armisteads are *nouveaux riches* from down south—not my kind of people." Without really changing the subject, she went on: "We've lived here for quite a long time, you know. My grandfather Falconer's ranch took in a good part of the coastal plain and the whole mountainside, all the way to the top of the first range. All I have left is a few hundred acres."

While I was trying to think of an appropriate comment, she said in a more immediate voice: "Stanley phoned me last night and asked me for fifteen hundred dollars cash, today."

"What for?"

"He said something vague, about buying information. As you may or may not know, my son is somewhat hipped on the subject of his father's desertion." Her voice was dry and careful.

"His wife told me that."

"Did she? It occurred to me that the fifteen hundred dollars might have something to do with you."

"It doesn't." I thought of Al, the pale man in the dark suit, but decided not to bring him up right now.

"Who's paying you?" the woman said rather sharply.

"I haven't been paid."

"I see." She sounded as if she distrusted what she saw. "Are you and my daughter-in-law good friends?"

"I met her this morning. We have friends in common."

"Then you probably know that Stanley and she have been close to breaking up. I never did think that their marriage would last."

"Why?"

"Jean is an intelligent girl but she comes from an entirely different class. I don't believe she's ever understood my son, though I've tried to explain something about our family traditions." She turned her head from the road to glance at me. "Is Stanley really interested in this blond girl?"

"Obviously he is, but maybe not in the way you mean. He wouldn't have brought your grandson along—"

"Don't be too sure of that. He brought Ronny because he knows I love the boy, and because he wants money from me. Remember when he found I wasn't here, he tried to leave Ronny with Fritz. I'd give a lot to know what they're up to."

II

At the base of a sandstone bluff where the road petered out entirely, she stopped the pickup and we got out.

"This is where we shift to shanks' mare," she said. "Ordinarily we could have driven around by way of Rattlesnake Road, but that's where they're fighting the fire."

In the lee of the bluff was a brown wooden sign, "Falconer Trail." The trail was a dusty track bulldozed out of the steep side of the canyon. As Mrs. Broadhurst went up ahead of me, she explained that her father had given the land for the trail to the Forest Service. She sounded as if she was trying to cheer herself in any way she could.

I ate her dust until I was looking down into the tops of the tallest sycamores in the canyon below. A daytime moon hung over the bluff, and we went on climbing toward it. When we reached the top I was wet under my clothes.

About a hundred yards back from the edge, a large weathered redwood cabin stood against a grove of trees. Some of the trees had been blackened and maimed where the fire had burned an erratic swath through the grove. The cabin itself was partly red and looked as if it had been splashed with blood.

Beyond the trees was a black hillside where the fire had browsed. The hillside slanted up to a ridge road and continued rising beyond the ridge to where the fire was now. It seemed to be moving laterally across the face of the mountain. The flames that from a distance had looked like artillery flashes were crashing through the thick chaparral like cavalry.

The ridge road was about midway between us and the main body of the fire. Toward the east, where the foothills flattened out into a mesa, the road curved down toward a collection of buildings which looked like a small college. Between them and the fire. bulldozers were crawling back and forth on the face of the mountain, cutting a firebreak in the deep brush.

The road was clogged with tanker trucks and other heavy equipment. Men stood around them in waiting attitudes, as if by behaving modestly and discreetly they could make the fire stay up on the mountain and die there, like an unwanted god.

As Mrs. Broadhurst and I approached the cabin I could see that part of its walls and roof had been splashed from the air with red fire retardant. The rest of the walls and the shutters over the windows were weathered gray.

The door was hanging open, with the key in the Yale lock. Mrs. Broadhurst walked up to it slowly, as if she dreaded what she might find inside. But there was nothing unusual to be seen in the big rustic front room. The ashes in the stone fireplace were cold, and might have been cold for years. Pieces of old-fashioned furniture draped with canvas stood around like formless images of the past.

Mrs. Broadhurst sat down heavily on a canvas-covered armchair. Dust rose around her. She coughed and spoke in a different voice, low and ashamed:

"I came up the trail a little too fast, I'm afraid."

I went out to the kitchen to get her some water. There were cups in the cupboard, but when I turned on the tap in the tin sink no water came. The butane stove was disconnected too.

I walked through the other rooms while I was at it: two downstairs bedrooms and a sleeping loft which was reached by steep wooden stairs. The loft was lit by a dormer window, and there were three beds in it, covered with canvas. One of them looked rumpled. I stripped the canvas off it. In the heavy gray blanket underneath there was a Rorschach blot of blood which looked recent but not fresh.

I went dow to the big front room. Mrs. Broadhurst had rested her head against the back of the chair. Her closed face was smooth and peaceful, and she was snoring gently.

92

I heard the rising roar of a plane coming in low over the mountain. I went out the back door in time to see its red spoor falling on the fire. The plane grew smaller, its roar dimuendoed.

Two deer—a doe and a fawn—came down the slope in a dry creek channel, heading for the grove. They saw me and rockinghorsed over a fallen log into the trees.

From the rear of the cabin a washed-out gravel lane overgrown with weeds meandered toward the ridge road. Starting along the lane toward the trees, I noticed wheel tracks in the weeds leading off toward a small stable. The wheel tracks looked new, and I could see only one set of them.

I followed them to the stable and peered in. A black convertible that looked like Stanley's stood there with the top down. I found the registration in the dash compartment. It was Stanley's all right.

I slammed the door of the convertible. A noise that sounded like an echo or a response came from the direction of the trees. Perhaps it was the crack of a stick breaking. I went out and headed for the partly burned grove. All I could hear was the sound of my own footsteps and a faint sighing which came from the wind in the trees.

Then I made out a more distant noise which I didn't recognize. It sounded like the whirring of wings. I felt hot wind on my face and glanced up the slope.

The wall of smoke that hung above the fire was leaning out from the mountain. At its base the fire was burning more brightly and had changed direction. Outriders of flame were leaping down the slope to the left, the firemen were moving along the ridge road to meet them.

The wind was changing. I could hear it rattling now among the leaves— the same sound that had wakened me in West Los Angeles early that morning. There were human noises, too—sounds of movement among the trees.

"Stanley?" I said.

A man in a blue suit and a red hard hat stepped out from behind the blotched trunk of a sycamore. He was a big man, and he moved with a kind of clumsy lightness.

"Looking for somebody?" He had a quiet cool voice, which gave the effect of holding itself in reserve.

"Several people."

"I'm the only one around," he said pleasantly.

His heavy arms and thighs bulged through his business clothes. His face was wet, as there was dirt on his shoes. He took off his hard hat, wiping his face and forehead with a bandanna handkerchief. His hair was gray and clipped short, like fur on a cannonball.

I walked toward him, into the skeletal shadow of the sycamore. The smoky moon was lodged in its top, segmented by small black branches. With a quick conjurer's motion, the big man produced a pack of cigarettes from his breast pocket and thrust it toward me.

"Smoke?"

"No thanks. I don't smoke."

"Don't smoke cigarettes, you mean?"

"I gave them up."

"What about cigars?"

"I never liked them," I said. "Are you taking a poll?"

"You might call it that." He smiled broadly, revealing several gold teeth. "How about cigarillos? Some people smoke them instead of cigarettes."

"I've noticed that."

"These people you say you're looking for, do any of them smoke cigarillos?"

"I don't think so." Then I remembered that Stanley Broadhurst did. "Why?"

"No reason, I'm just curious." He glanced up the mountainside. "That fire is starting to move. I don't like the feel of the wind. It has the feel of a Santa Ana."

"It was blowing down south early this morning."

"So I've heard. Are you from Los Angeles?"

"That's right." He seemed to have all the time he needed, but I was tired of fooling around with him. "My name is Archer. I'm a licensed private detective, employed by the Broadhurst family."

94

"I was wondering. I saw you come out of the stable."

"Stanley Broadhurst's car is there."

"I know," he said. "Is Stanley Broadhurst one of the people you're looking for?"

"Yes, he is."

"License?"

I showed him my photostat.

"Well, I may be able to help you."

He turned abruptly and moved in among the trees along a rutted trail. I followed him. The leaves were so dry under my feet that it was like walking on corn flakes.

We came to an opening in the trees. The big sycamore which partly overarched it had been burned. Smoke was still rising from its charred branches and from the undergrowth behind it.

Near the middle of the open space there was a hole in the ground between three and four feet in diameter. A space stood upright beside it in a pile of dirt and stones. Off to one side of the pile, a pickax lay on the ground. Its sharp tip seemed to have been dipped in dark red paint. Reluctantly I looked down into the hole.

In its shallow depth a man's body lay curled like a foetus, face up-turned. I recognized his peppermint-striped shirt, glad rags to be buried in. And in spite of the dirt that stuffed his open mouth and clung to his eyes, I recognized Stanley Broadhurst, and I said so.

The big man absorbed the information quietly. "What was he doing here, do you know?"

"No, I don't. But I believe this is part of his family's ranch. You haven't explained what you're doing here."

"I'm with the Forest Service. My name's Joe Kelsey, I'm trying to find out what started this fire. And," he added deliberately, "I think I have found out. It seems to have flared up in this immediate area. I came across *this*, right there." He indicated a yellow plastic marker stuck in the burned-over ground a few feet from where we were standing. Then he produced a small aluminum evidence case and snapped it open. It contained a single half-burned cigarillo.

"Did Broadhurst smoke these?"

"I saw him smoke one this morning. You'll probably find the package in his clothes."

"Yeah, but I didn't want to move him until the coroner sees him. It looks as if I may have to, though."

He squinted uphill toward the fire. It blazed like a displaced sunset through the trees. The black silhouettes of men fighting it looked small and futile in spite of their tanker trucks and bulldozers. Off to the left the fire had spilled over the ridge and was pouring downhill like fuming acid eating the dry brush. Its smoke blew ahead of it and spread across the city toward the sea.

Kelsey took the spade and started to throw dirt into the hole, talking as he worked.

"I hate to bury a man twice, but it's better than letting him get roasted. The fire's coming back this way."

"Was he buried when you found him?"

"That's correct. But whoever buried him didn't do much of a job covering up. I found the spade and the pick with the blood on it—and then the filled hole with loose dirt around. So I started digging. I didn't know what I was going to find. But I sort of had a feeling that it would be a dead man with a hole in his head."

Kelsey worked rapidly. The dirt covered Stanley's striped shirt and his upturned insulted face. Kelsey spoke to me over his shoulder."

"You mentioned that you were looking for several people. Who are the others?"

"The dead man's little boy is one. And there was a blond girl with him."

"So I've heard. Can you describe her?"

"Blue eyes, five foot six, 115 pounds, age about eighteen. Broadhurst's widow can tell you more about her. She's at the ranchhouse.

"Where's your car? I came out on a fire truck."

I told him that Stanley's mother had brought me in her pickup, and that she was in the cabin. Kelsey stopped spading dirt. His face was running with sweat, and mildly puzzled.

"What's she doing in there?"

"Resting."

"We're going to have to interrupt her rest."

Beyond the grove, in the unburned brush, the fire had grown almost as tall as the trees. The air moved in spurts and felt like hot animal breath.

We ran away from it, with Kelsey carrying the spade and me carrying the bloody pick. The pick felt heavy by the time we reached the door of the cabin. I set it down and knocked on the door before I went in.

Mrs. Broadhurst sat up with a start. Her face was rosy. Sleep clung to her eyes and furred her voice:

"I must have dozed off, forgive me, but I had the sweetest dream. I spent—we spent our honeymoon here, you know, right in this cabin. It was during the war, quite early in the war and traveling wasn't possible. I dreamed that I was on my honeymoon, and none of the bad things had happened."

Her half-dreaming eyes focused on my face and recognized the signs, which I couldn't conceal, of another bad thing that had happened. Then she saw Kelsey with the spade in his hands. He looked like a giant gravedigger blocking the light in the doorway.

Mrs. Broadhurst's normal expression, competent and cool and rather strained, forced itself down over her open face. She got up very quickly, and almost lost her balance.

"Mr. Kelsey? It's Mr. Kelsey, isn't it? What's happened?"

"We found your son, ma'am."

"Where is he? I want to talk to him."

Kelsey said in deep embarrassment: "I'm afraid that won't be possible, ma'am."

"Why? Has he gone somewhere?"

Kelsey gave me an appealing look. Mrs. Broadhurst walked toward him.

"What are you doing with that spade? That's my spade, isn't it?"

"I wouldn't know, ma'am."

She took it out of his hands. "It most certainly is. I bought it for my own use last spring. Where did you get hold of it, from my gardener?"

"I found it in the clump of trees yonder." Kelsey gestured in that direction.

'What on earth was it doing there?"

Kelsey's mouth opened and shut. He was unwilling or afraid to tell her that Stanley was dead. I moved toward her and told her that her son had been killed, probably with a pickax.

I stepped outside and showed her the pickax. "Is this yours, too?"

She looked at it dully. "Yes, I believe it is."

Her voice was a low monotone, hardly more than a whisper. She turned and began to run toward the burning trees, stumbling in her high-heeled riding boots. Kelsey ran after her, heavily and rapidly like a bear. He took her around the waist and lifted her off her feet and turned her around away from the fire.

She kicked and shouted: "Let me go. I want my son."

"He's in a hole in the ground, ma'am. You can't go in there now, nobody can. But his body won't burn. It's safe underground."

She twisted in his arms and struck at his face. He dropped her. She fell in the brown weeds, beating at the ground and crying that she wanted her son.

I got down on my knees beside her and talked her into getting up and coming with us. We went down the trail in single file, with Kelsey leading the way and Mrs. Broadhurst between us. I stayed close behind her, in case she tried to do something wild like throwing herself down the side of the bluff. She moved passively with her head down, like a prisoner between guards.

III

Kelsey carried the spade in one hand and the bloody pickax in the other. He tossed them into the back of the truck and helped Mrs. Broadhurst into the cab. I took the wheel.

She rode between us in silence, looking straight ahead along the stony road. She didn't utter a sound until we turned at her mailbox into the avocado grove. Then she let out a gasp which sounded as if she'd been holding her breath all the way down the canyon.

"Where is my grandson?"

"We don't know," Kelsey said.

"You mean that he's dead, too. Is that what you mean?"

Kelsey took refuge in a southwestern drawl which helped to soften his answer. "I mean that nobody's seen hide nor hair of him, ma'am."

"What about the blond girl? Where is she?"

"I only wish I knew."

"Did she kill my son?"

"It looks like it, ma'am. It looks like she hit him over the head with that pickax."

"And buried him?"

"He was buried when I found him."

"How could a girl do that?"

"It was a shallow grave, ma'am. Girls can do about anything boys can do when they set their minds to it."

A whine had entered Kelsey's drawl under the pressure of the questioning and the greater pressure of her fear. Impatiently she turned to me:

"Mr. Archer, is my grandson Ronny dead?"

"No." I said it with some force, to beat back the possibility that he was.

"Has that girl abducted him?"

"It's a good assumption to work on. But they may simply have run away from the fire."

"You know that isn't so." She sounded as if she had crossed a watershed in her life, beyond which nothing good could happen.

I stopped the pickup behind my car on the driveway. Kelsey got out and offered to help Mrs. Broadhurst. She pushed his hands away. But she climbed out like a woman overtaken by sudden age.

"You can park the truck in the carport," she said to me. "I don't like to leave it out in the sun."

"Excuse me," Kelsey said, "but you might as well leave it out here. The fire's coming down the canyon, and it may get to your house. I'll help you bring your things out if you like, and drive one of your cars."

Mrs. Broadhurst cast a slow look around the house and its surroundings. "There's never been fire in this canyon in my lifetime."

"That means it's ripe," he said. "The brush up above is fifteen and twenty feet deep, and as dry as a chip. This is a fifty-year fire. It could take your house unless the wind changes again."

"Then let it."

Jean came to meet us at the door, a little tardily, as if she dreaded what we were going to say. I told her that her husband was dead and that her son was missing. The two women exchanged a questioning look, as if each of them was looking into the other for the source of all their troubles. Then they came together in the doorway and stood in each other's arms.

Kelsey came up behind me on the porch. He tipped his hard hat and spoke to the younger woman, who was facing him over Mrs. Broadhurst's shoulder.

"Mrs. Stanley Broadhurst?"

"Yes."

"I understand you can give me a description of the girl who was with your husband."

"I can try."

She separated herself from the older woman, who went into the house. Jean rested on the railing near the hummingbird feeder. A hummingbird buzzed her. She moved to the other side of the porch and sat on a canvas chair, leaning forward in a strained position and repeating for Kelsey her description of the blue-eyed girl with the strange eyes.

"And you say she's eighteen or so?"

Jean nodded. Her reactions were quick but mechanical, as if her mind was focused somewhere else.

"Is—was your husband interested in her, Mrs. Broadhurst?"

"Obviously he was," she said in a dry bitter voice. "But I gathered she was more interested in my son."

"Interested in what way?"

"I don't know what way."

Kelsey switched to a less sensitive line of questioning. "How was she dressed?"

"Last night she had on a sleeveless yellow dress. I didn't see her this morning."

"I did," I put in. "She was still wearing the yellow dress. I assume you'll be giving all this to the police."

"Yessir, I will. Right now I want to talk to the gardener. He may be able to tell us how that spade and pick got up on the mountain. What's his name?"

"Frederick Snow—we call him Fritz," Jean said. "He isn't here."

"Where is he?"

"He rode Stanley's old bicycle down the road about half an hour ago, when the wind changed. He wanted to take the Cadillac, but I told him not to."

"Doesn't he have a car of his own?"

"I believe he has some kind of jalopy."

"Where is it?"

She shrugged slightly. "I don't know."

"Where was Fritz this morning?"

"I can't tell you. He seems to have been the only one here for most of the morning."

Kelsey's face saddened. "How does he get along with your little boy?"

"Fine." Then his meaning entered her eyes and darkened them. She shook her head as if to deny the meaning, dislodge the darkness. "Fritz wouldn't hurt Ronny, he's always been kind to him."

"Then why did he take off?"

"He said that he was worried about his mother. But I think he was scared of the fire. He was almost crying."

"So am I scared of the fire," Kelsey said. "It's why I'm in this business."

"Are you a policeman?" Jean said. "Is that why you're asking me all these questions?"

"I'm with the Forest Service, assigned to investigate the causes of fires. "He dug into an inside pocket, produced the aluminum evidence case, and showed her the half-burned cigarillo. "Does this look like one of you husband's?"

"Yes it does. But surely you're not trying to prove that he started it. What's the point if he's dead?" Her voice had risen a little out of control.

"The point is this. Whoever killed him probably made him drop this in the dry grass. That means they're legally and financially responsible for the fire. And it's my job to establish the facts. Where does this man Snow live?"

"With his mother. I think their house is quite near here. My mother-in-law can tell you. Mrs. Snow used to work for her."

We found Mrs. Broadhurst in the living room, standing at a corner window which framed the canyon. The room was so large that she looked small at the far end of it. She didn't turn when we moved up to her.

She was watching the progress of the fire. It was in the head of the canyon now, slipping downhill like a loose volcano, and spouting smoke and sparks above the treetops. The eucalyptus trees behind the house were momentarily blanched by the gusty winds. The blackbirds and pigeons had all gone.

Kelsey and I exchanged glances. It was time that we went, too. I let him do the talking, since it was his territory and his kind of emergency. He addressed the woman's unmoving back.

"Mrs. Broadhurst? Don't you think we better get out of here?"

"You go. Please do go. I'm staying, for the present."

"You can't do that. That fire is really on its way."

She turned on him. Her face had sunk on its bones; it made her look old and formidable.

"Don't tell me what I can or can't do. I was born in this house. I've never lived anywhere else. If the house goes, I might as well go with it. Everything else has gone."

"You're not serious, ma'am."

"Am I not?"

"You don't want to get yourself burned, do you?"

"I think I'd almost welcome the flames. I'm very cold, Mr. Kelsey."

Her tone was tragic, but there was a note of hysteria running through it, or something worse. A stubbornness which could mean that her mind had slipped a notch, and stuck at a crazy angle.

Kelsey cast a desperate look around the room. It was full of Victorian furniture, with dark Victorian portraits on the walls, and several cabinets full of stuffed native birds under glass.

"Don't you want to save your things, ma'am? Your silver and bird specimens and pictures and mementos?"

She spread her hands in a hopeless gesture as if everything had long since run through them. Kelsey was getting nowhere trying to sell her back the pieces of her life.

I said:

"We need your help, Mrs. Broadhurst."

She looked at me in mild surprise. "My help?"

"Your grandson is missing. This is a bad time and place for a little boy to be lost—"

"It's a judgment on me."

"That's nonsense."

"So I'm talking nonsense, am I?"

I disregarded her angry question. "Fritz the gardener may know where he is. I believe you know his mother. Is that correct?"

Her answer came slowly. "Edna Snow used to be my housekeeper. You can't seriously believe that Fritz—" she stopped, unwilling to put her question into words.

"It would be a great help if you'd come along and talk to Fritz and his mother."

"Very well, I will."

We drove out the lane like a funeral cortege. Mrs. Broadhurst was leading in her Cadillac. Jean and I came next in the green Mercedes. Kelsey brought up the rear, driving the pickup.

I looked back from the mailbox. Sparks and embers were blowing down the canyon, plunging into the trees behind the house like bright exotic birds taking the place of the birds that had flown.

SANTA BARBARA, 1970

I wake from an afternoon nap not
knowing who I am
walking out on the terrace, seeing
a strange city, built on the western seaboard of a
continent, under a foreign light of blue
weather one would never expect of a familiar place.

The lights are on before it's dark.
This is not home, this is some minor city of Japan,
provincial coast of France, a Black-Sea town, or
some forgotten port looking on the Galápagos.

I with my moustache, my beard, my flared trousers and
knitted sweater, my unnatural sleeping at noon, my
yawns and my strange thoughts, am
an inhabitant, an
inexplicable local of this foreign land.

Frederick Turner
— *1970*

Robert Easton (b. 1915) is one of the most genuinely local of Santa Barbara writers, having grown up in the area before going off to Harvard. Both his fiction and nonfiction works reflect his interest in western history. His account of the 1969 oil spill, Black Tide *(1972) is a valuable addition to local history writing.*

BLOW OUT

THE DAY BEGAN with patches of blue sky and some sun, but the tops of the mountains that rose abruptly behind Santa Barbara, California, were covered with clouds, following heavy rains, and so were the tops of the mountains on the islands twenty miles off shore. The islands—Anacapa, Santa Cruz, Santa Rosa, San Miguel—lay in an east-west line paralleling the mainland for more than sixty miles. They looked like foreign lands, blue and mysterious in the rainwashed air. As rain squalls passed over the Santa Barbara Channel, they hid the islands from onshore observers. They also hid offshore drilling Platforms A and B, recently emplaced by the Union Oil Company five and a half miles from the city's waterfront.

The city, famous for its beauty and charm, lay on a slope between low foothills facing the sea. From harbor and palm-tree-lined beaches, its one main thoroughfare, State Street, ran up three miles to a crest near the old Spanish mission. Its downtown buildings were low-rise. Many, such as the City Hall and *News-Press* buildings in the central square were of stucco and tile, as were many of the houses set in the trees and gardens of the hillsides.

About seventy-five thousand people lived in Santa Barbara and as many more lived in the adjacent communities of Montecito, Summerland,

and Carpinteria on the east and Goleta and Isla Vista on the west. Most of them depended on their natural environment in some way for a living.

Tourism was the area's economic base. More than four million people came every year to enjoy mountains, beaches, oceans, and islands, and the gentle climate. But there were also research and development industries, residential and retirement facilities, medical centers, a campus of the University of California, commercial and sports fishing, some lemon and avocado groves, and, lately, offshore oil.

At 7:25 A.M. William R. (Bill) Robinson arrived at the Union Oil Company dock at the Navy Pier near the foot of the breakwater ready to board the work boat that would take him and some forty other building-trades-workers—pipe fitters, electricians, sheet metal workers—to Platform A, where they were completing piping and wiring of the huge structure. Like others assembling in the gray cool morning, Robinson was middle-aged. He had a wife, three children in school, and had chosen Santa Barbara for his home because he liked the climate and atmosphere. He disliked channel oil development, which seemed a threat to the city's natural surroundings, but the money to be made on the platforms—as much as $1,320 weekly including overtime—overcame his objections. He wore work boots and Windbreaker jacket and carried a lunch pail. His hard hat and his tools were waiting for him on Platform A.

As the work boat was leaving the harbor, Lieutenant George H. Brown, III, entered his office in U.S. Coast Guard Group Headquarters on the waterfront, a stone's throw from Union's dock. The one-story cinder-block building was the same size and had the same appearance as the public rest room nearby. The city had built both buildings and leased one to the Coast Guard. Brown's office occupied nearly half its usable interior. The other half was crammed with teletype, radio equipment, lockers, a desk, and a head. Brown, a stocky, bright-eyed young man of twenty-seven, a former Sea Scout from Braintree, Massachusetts, had recently commanded a cutter in Vietnam coastal waters. As Commander Coast Guard Group,

Santa Barbara, his responsibilities included 150 miles of coastline from Point Dume, south of Oxnard, northward around the continental corner at Point Conception to the mouth of the Santa Maria River. In this area he was responsible for search and rescue missions; enforcement of federal laws; safety standards for yachts, motorboats, and other noncommercial vessels; supervision of Coast Guard installations at Conception, Arguello, Anacapa Island, and Port Hueneme; and pollution control.

Lieutenant Brown was wearing a blue winter uniform this morning which exactly resembled that of the Navy except for the buttons. For the past three days he had been tramping rain-swept beaches and telephoning oil companies to determine the source of oil that had come ashore at Rincon, eighteen miles southeast of Santa Barbara. It was low-gravity crude in moderate amounts. After talking with State Fish and Game Department representatives concerned with pollution in state waters, Brown has concluded the oil came from pipes and sumps on the mainland broken open by recent floods and not from offshore platforms.

There were twelve drilling platforms scattered along the coast for fifty miles. Eight stood in state water, within three miles from shore. Four, including Union's two new ones, stood in so-called federal water, between the three- and twelve-mile limits. Union was operating Platform A and B for a group that included Gulf Oil Corporation, Mobil Oil Corporation, and Texaco Incorporated. The federal government had leased the consortium the right to drill on the 54,000 ocean-floor acres of Federal Lease Tract 402, in return for $61,418,000 in cash, plus a royalty of one-sixth market price barrel of oil produced, and an annual rental of $16,2000 for the tract.

With its larger partners, Union hoped to develop an oil field under Platform A and B that would improve its tenuous position in or near the top "big ten" of a fiercely competitive industry. Conglomerates were the order of the day, but Union did not want to be conglomerated. With assets of $2.4 billion, the Union Oil Company of California was struggling for its independence. It was the eleventh largest oil company in the United States. It had been founded in the Santa Barbara Channel area, but its operations now extended from Alaska to Indonesia, to Hong Kong, to Louisiana, to Chicago, and to many other parts of the world. It operated petrochemical companies and huge tankers. It manufactured fireplace briquets and agricultural fertilizers. It was a modern industrial giant.

Union's two controversial new platforms lay opposite a community that had been founded by a Spanish settlement in the late 1700s and peopled later largely by New Englanders. Ironically in the light of what was to happen, Santa Barbara had been named for Saint Barbara of Nicomedia, the patron saint of petroleum.

The community's psychic life, as well as its economic life, was largely centered on its natural surroundings including the great oaks and sycamores that grew down its canyons to the water's edge. For forty years Santa Barbarans had had an architectural board of review to see that downtown buildings harmonized with good taste. They had banned billboards, high-rise buildings, and urban sprawl, and had fought off an elevated freeway that would have risen like a technological spite fence between them and their seascape. They had bought and beautified five miles of beach front as a public park, and they had resisted oil development, onshore and offshore, as their Puritan forefathers had resisted the devil.

Present-day Santa Barbarans, against offshore oil drilling in general, had particularly opposed Union's two new platforms as an immediate threat to the city's tourist and recreation industries and to the area's ecology. With their drilling towers, Platforms A and B rose as high above the water as twenty-story buildings and their potential for environmental disruption loomed as large as their silhouettes on a clear day. A virtual forest of seventy similar platforms and about four thousand wells was the appalling prospect for the channel's federal water. In response to citizen protests, government and industry spokesmen had given assurances that this vast development would be managed without adverse effect. Modern technology would provide the answers. "You have nothing to fear," Secretary of the Interior Stewart L. Udall had promised Santa Barbarans two years earlier, when the federal leases were proposed, "no leases will be granted except under conditions that will protect your environment."

108

On Platform A, Well A-21 had been drilled to its maximum depth of 3,479 feet and the crew was removing the drill pipe from the hole. The platform stood in 188 feet of water. The top of its vertical drilling rig reached 210 feet above the surface of the sea. Its structural framework of steel pipes weighed about 3,000 tons. Steel pilings inside its hollow legs had been driven into the ocean floor to stabilize it against wind, wave, and earthquake. Its superstructure supported two 115- by 134-foot decks, drilling slots for 56 wells, a galley and lounge, sleeping quarters for a dozen men, workshop, and a helipad. There was in addition to a slant-drilling rig, protruding at an angle of about 30 degrees, for tapping oil sands that lay too near the ocean floor to be tapped by the vertical rig. A 34,000-volt submarine cable brought power to the platform from shore, and a submarine pipeline was already to carry its petroleum to onshore processing plants. Platform A had cost about $5 million. Each of its 56 wells would cost about a quarter million more.

Under the vertical rig, the crew was pulling up the drill pipe so that electrical recordings of the geological formations penetrated by the hole could be made. Then the entire hole would be protected with steel casing, as the upper 239 feet already were. Well A-21 had been drilled in only fourteen days. Penetrating rapidly through shallow oil-bearing sands and shales, a 12-¼-inch-diameter steel-alloy bit rotating at the end of the 4-½-inch-diameter drill pipe had reached a deeper oil horizon. Drilling mud—a viscous grayish-colored-chemical fluid of high specific gravity—circulating down through the pipe out through apertures in the bit, and up through the annulus—the space between the drill pipe and the sides of the hole—had prevented the bit from overheating under the tremendous pressure of pipe from above and the resistance of earth from below. The drilling mud had plastered the walls of the hole and prevented them from caving, and it had carried the bit's cuttings to the surface. But the most important thing it had done was to balance the pressure of oil or gas encountered during drilling.

Oil well drilling requires a balancing act: man-made (mud-made) pressure from above versus earth-made pressures from below.

109

Sometimes this balance is upset by the use of a drilling mud that is too light in weight. Sometimes it is upset by pulling up the drill pipe too fast. The result is a blowout: an uncontrolled eruption of gas or oil.

By 10:45 A.M on January 28 the crew employed by Union's drilling contractor, Peter Bawden Drilling Incorporated, had removed seven "stands"—seven 90-foot lengths of drill pipe—from the hole and set them in racks at the side of the rig. The first five stands had "pulled tight," indicating that mud and debris might be clogging the hole, but the next two pulled freely. As each successive stand was hauled up into the derrick by the traveling block, the drilling crew unscrewed it at the rotary table at deck level. They were in the act of disconnecting the eighth stand when Bill Robinson, working nearby, heard a loud hissing roar that filled him with instant alarm. He looked up and saw dark gray mud mixed with gas shoot out the top of stand number eight, ninety feet above the deck, and cascade down upon men and equipment. The crew hastily finished disconnecting the eighth stand and set it in the racks. As they did so, mud and gas shot with a deafening roar from the open pit at their feet and rose twenty feet or more into the derrick. Well A-21 had blown out, and the largest disaster of its kind in U.S. history had begun.

Margaret Millar (1915-1994) did not achieve the fame that her husband Kenneth Millar did, but she was admired by those who appreciated good writing. Like him, many of her suspense novels use Santa Barbara settings. Her paean to birding, The Birds and Beasts Were There *(1967), is a first person account of the Coyote fire.*

THE COYOTE FIRE

IT WAS THE FIRST DAY OF AUTUMN, 1964. Those Santa Barbara residents who lived within a block or two of the sea woke up to a dense fog and the ominous warnings of the foghorn at the end of the breakwater. The rest of the city was awakened by the brilliant rays of a September sun and realized it was going to be a hot day. How hot none of us could ever have guessed.

The summer that was ending had been one of drought, as usual. The last rain measurable on our gauge was a tenth of an inch in May. September occasionally brings some moisture—the hundred-year average is about a quarter of an inch—but it is better known for bringing our hottest and driest days. For us this is the month of santanas, the scorching winds that blow in over the mountains from the Mojave Desert, a vast area covering some 13,000 square miles.

We are accustomed to sea winds and their ravages: tons of kelp strewn along the beaches, alive with tiny octopi and starfish and skate eggs that look like black plastic comb cases; boats escaped from their moorings, loose anchors and racing buoys, dead fish and sea lions and leopard sharks; battered sea birds, surf scoters and whitewings, all kinds of gulls and terns and cormorants, western grebes and horned grebes, arctic loons and red-throated loons; and once—and only once, thank Heaven—the newly severed head of an enormous wild boar, brought to my reluctant attention by our German shepherd, Brandy.

Sea winds may be violent and cruel, but in a coastal town they are a natural part of life. Santanas are strangers, intruders from the other side of the mountains. They are not polite or kindly strangers. We give them no welcome and they in turn come bearing no good will. One of them almost cost our city its life.

A santana ordinarily arrives on a calm, quiet night. Some people claim it gives no warning, others sense its approach or "feel it in their bones." Nothing psychic is involved, and no bones either, merely skin and mucous membranes reacting to a rapid lowering of humidity and rise in temperature. In southern California the temperature always goes down with the sun, and this rule is broken only by the arrival of a santana.

On one of these calm, quiet nights in September, a person may become suddenly aware that changes are taking place. There is a rustle of leaves, the squawk of a gate swinging, the bang of a screen door. A gust of wind roars down the canyon, and the eucalyptus trees begin to writhe. Leaves begin rushing past the windows like refugees fleeing the forest, and the hard little seed pods of the tea tree tap the glass like animals' claws. If, at this stage of the game, all doors and windows are locked, drapes pulled, and the drafts of fireplaces closed tight, it won't do much good. The dust seems to penetrate the very walls, and every flat surface in the house is soon covered with it. Skin is taut, throats parched, eyes gritty, tempers short. In a santana the milk of human kindness dries up like everything else.

In general, sea winds are fairly strong and steady, and desert winds come in gusts. Sometimes both are blowing simultaneously and between gusts of the desert wind the sea wind rushes in. Then there begins a tug of war between them with the city caught in the middle, a nervous referee for a battle of giants who haven't read the rule book. Temperatures go up and down so rapidly thermometers haven't time to register them accurately— and the range is wide, fifty or sixty degrees.

By sunrise the battle is over, the friendly wind is resting, the stranger has fled, the cleanup begins. Branches and leaves, and the litter blown out of overturned trash cans must be picked up; trees and shrubs and flowers must be hosed down to remove the dust that clogs their breathing pores; damaged bird feeders must be fixed and rehung, and the dirt and debris cleaned out of the bird baths. If we're lucky, the stranger won't come back the next night...

The morning of September 22 was windless. The heavy fog that had blanketed the coastal area at dawn was burned off by the sun before nine o'clock and the mercury in the official temperature gauge, which is located at the shore, began to rise rapidly, up through the seventies into the eighties. Our area, at an elevation of about 550 feet was a good deal hotter, a situation that was reversed only on very rare occasions.

I had watered heavily the previous afternoon, using the rainbirds on the roof in spite of the outraged protests of the scrub jays. We had these roof sprinklers installed several years before by an off-duty fireman after the Montecito fire chief had urged all hill and canyon dwellers to be prepared for an emergency as the layers of brushwood grew higher and thicker and more dangerous. The emergency hadn't occurred, but we used the rainbirds to cool the house and to water a considerable part of our property. Few people had taken the fire chief's advice. Rainbirds on a roof were so uncommon that at first when we used ours, passing motorists would stop and stare, and one even inquired if we'd broken a water main. If the effect was peculiar from the outside, it was doubly peculiar to sit inside and listen to rain pounding on the shingles, to see it pelting the windows and gushing out of the eaves troughs, while just beyond the walls of water a brilliant sun shone from an unclouded sky. Ordering up a private rainstorm in the midst of a California summer is as close to playing God as I care to come.

But the three rainbirds, even twirling full tilt, were no match for the September heat and drought. All traces of moisture had disappeared by midmorning the next day, and the temperature was in the nineties and still rising. The birds coped with the heat in several ways. The yellowthroats napped in a sheltered spot down by the creek. Some of the English sparrows and blackbirds cooled themselves by breathing rapidly through open beaks. The hooded orioles and Anna's hummingbirds drank nectar from the golden hearts of the trumpet flowers and mockers crushed the ripening elderberries and eugenias. The wrentits kept in the shade, foraging in the dense poison oak that was reddening the canyon slopes. All half dozen bird baths were in continual use, the champion bathers being the house finches, who looked like miniature rainbirds as they hurled water madly in every direction at once.

* * *

Elsewhere in the country the Warren Commission was still weighing the evidence against Lee Harvey Oswald; L.B.J. predicted tax cuts to the Steelworkers' Union; Goldwater hit the campaign trail in Oklahoma; the Phils were 5-1/2 games up on the Cincinnati Reds; and Napa County in northern California had been declared a disaster area by Governor Brown after a forest fire had burned ninety square miles and was still raging out of control. One section of it was traveling at a rate of more than a mile an hour.

For some time Ken and I had been planning to buy an acre or two and eventually build a house. Every now and then when a new parcel of land came on the market we would make arrangements through a real estate agent to inspect it. That morning at eleven a young man took us out to see three acres in the foothills at the opposite end of Montecito. The owner, John Van Bergen, an architect, lived with his wife on the adjoining property in a house he'd recently designed and built himself.

We admired the Van Bergen house and its magnificent panorama of miles and miles of coastline. The region was somewhat higher than where we were living—which meant that it was more than somewhat hotter and dryer—and the terrain was steep. But my main objection to the place was that fact that it would not support an abundance of bird life. There was no source of water nearby, and the vegetation was limited to those native plants which could tolerate prolonged periods of drought, various types of shrubs which are usually grouped together under the name chaparral, and a few small live oak trees.

I had another objection. The climate, in conjunction with many years' accumulation of underbrush, made the place an even greater fire hazard than a wooded canyon like ours. If the Van Bergens, newcomers from Chicago, realized this they didn't show it. Neither did the insurance companies. In response to my question Mr. Van Bergen said they paid the same insurance premiums as anyone else, though certain precautions against fire had been built into the house, such as a flat roof which held a three-inch layer of water.

It was one o'clock when we left the Van Bergens. We drove down to the beach club, had a cold lunch and headed for the surf. On the ramp to the beach I was detained by a friend who wanted to ask me a bird question, and it was here that one of the lifeguards from the pool caught up with me. A message had just been received in the office from Richmond Miller, the young, newly elected president of the Santa Barbara Audubon Society. Rich, failing to reach us at home, had called the beach club to leave word that a fire had been reported on Coyote Road below Mountain Drive. He didn't know how big a fire it was, but in that area, in that weather, even a glowworm was dangerous.

I thought of the fire raging through Napa County, traveling more than a mile an hour; the intersection of Coyote Road and Mountain Drive was half a mile crows' flight from our house. From where I was standing I could see the smoke rising in the air, black and brown and gray, changing color with the fire's fuel. I asked the lifeguard to call Ken in from the sea and tell him we had to go home.

At 2:02 P.M. smoke had been reported in the Coyote Road-Mountain Drive region by an unidentified woman. A minute later an off-duty fireman living in the area confirmed the report and the Coyote fire, as it came to be known, officially began its long and dreadful journey.

Its initial direction was up. At 2:23 it jumped Mountain Drive and the first houses in its path began burning. By 2:30 two planes were dropping fire-retardant chemicals. On the way home we could see the stuff falling like puffs of pink clouds out of a technicolor dream. Fire Retardant Pink was to become, in certain parts of Santa Barbara, the fashionable shade worn by many of the luckier houses, garages, cars, boats, corrals, horses, burros, dogs, cats, people, and at least one highly indignant peacock. The reddish color, by the way, was deliberately added to the formula to make hits and misses more apparent.

When Ken and I pulled into our driveway we met Bertha Blomstrand, the widow who lived across the road from us. She'd come over to check the whereabouts of our dogs in case they might have to be released, and to turn on the rainbirds. Bertha's action was the kind that typified people's attitude toward the fire right from the beginning: it was going to be a bad one and we were all in it together. The three of us stood watching the blaze and the smoke half a mile away, and listening to the shriek of sirens, the rhythmic clatter of the rainbirds and the roar of the borate bombers as they followed the sporty little yellow lead plane that showed them where to drop their loads. It was to be some time before the ordinary quiet sounds of an ordinary day were heard on our street again.

From our living room we saw houses on Mountain Drive burning unchecked. Wind-driven sparks landed in a large grove of eucalyptus and the oil-rich trees virtually exploded into flames. One of the houses in the direct path of the fire had been built by a local writer, Bill Richardson, for his family. It seemed certain to be destroyed, but at the last crucial moment a borate bomber scored a miraculously lucky hit and the place was saved along with a pet burro, four dogs and all of Bill's manuscripts.

It was three o'clock.

During the next hour men who'd served in World War II were surprised by the sudden appearance of an old army buddy, a B-17 Flying Fortress which had been sent down from Chino in northern California carrying 2000 gallons of fire-retardant fluid. By this time half a dozen other planes had arrived from Los Angeles as well as some helicopters, each capable of carrying 50 gallons of the fluid. A combination heliport and firecamp was set up on the athletic field of Westmont College, a private coeducational institution whose property line was two hundred yards from our own. Late afternoon also brought the first carloads of sightseers, the first wave of telephone calls and the first outbreak of contradictory rumors:

A storm front was heading our way from Oregon and rain would start any minute. No rain was in sight for a week.

Firefighters were coming from every part of the southwest, including the famed Zuni Indian crews from New Mexico, and the fire would be under control within a few hours. No firefighters could be spared because so many other areas were highly flammable, and the entire city of Santa Barbara was doomed.

Every household was to soak his roof, walls, shrubbery and trees. Water was to be conserved to keep the pressure from dropping.

We were spared a great many rumors because our only radio wasn't in working condition. The lack of communication proved to be a blessing in disguise. There was an advantage in not knowing exactly how bad things were until they were over.

As for the phone calls, it was gratifying to receive so many offers of sanctuary, some from people we hadn't been in contact with for years. Yet, as the hours passed and the phone kept ringing, we began to look on it as an insatiable monster demanding our continuous attention. The news it gave us in return was mostly bad—the fire was still going up the mountain, but it was also moving rapidly southward, in our direction, and two hundred acres were burned, including the houses of several people we knew. The only piece of good news was the information about the borate bomber saving Bill Richardson's place with a direct hit of fire retardant.

* * *

As the afternoon wore on and workers began leaving their jobs for the day, the stream of cars on our narrow little road increased. What kind of people were in these cars? I will quote one of them and let the reader judge for himself. A young man pulled into our driveway and shouted at Ken who was on the roof readjusting a rainbird:

"Hey, how do we get to the houses that are already burning?"

Darkness fell. At least it should have been darkness, but on the mountains a strange, misplaced and molten sun was rising and expanding, changing the landscape into a firescape. Instead of the normal quiet sounds of night there was the constant deafening roar of helicopters landing and taking off from the camp on the Westmont College athletic field. The borate bombers had stopped at dusk because they couldn't operate over the difficult terrain in the dark, and without chemicals to impede its progress the fire was spreading in all directions at once.

* * *

During the early part of the evening the hundreds fighting the fire and the thousands watching it never really doubted that it could and would be brought under control. Then at nine o'clock, the eventuality which some of us had been secretly dreading suddenly came. The first gust of a santana rushed down from the crest of the mountain, driving the flames before it like teams of dragons. It soon became obvious that the fire was going beyond the control of men and machines. If it was to be stopped it would have to be stopped by nature herself. Not only was it spreading at a fantastic speed, it was being forced by the santana to backtrack, destroying whatever had been missed or only half burned the first time.

That night Bill Richardson's house, miraculously saved by a borate bomber in midafternoon, burned to the ground.

The stream of sightseers continued. Our street, Chelham Way, is a circle, it goes nowhere, so only a very small percentage of the cars passing were on legitimate business. One of these stopped at the entrance to our driveway and the man behind the wheel asked us how to get to a house in the neighborhood where an elderly woman lived alone and might need help. He added, "Aren't you Mrs. Millar?"

I said I was.

"We met this morning. You were at our house looking at the acreage we have for sale."

It was John van Bergen and his wife. Less than twelve hours previously, we'd been talking to them about fire insurance rates and I'd been surprised to learn that they didn't have to pay higher premiums than we did.

There was no time to discuss the ironies of fate. We gave the Van Bergens the information they wanted and they drove on. Later that night they telephoned and offered us refuge from the fire, but by that time we'd decided that if we were forced to evacuate we would go to Ping and Jo Ferry's. We had a number of good reasons for our choice, perhaps the chief one being that when Jo Ferry called she had particularly invited our three dogs to come too. Many people had indicated willingness to take us into their homes, but they didn't especially want to entertain a dour and elderly Scottie, a nervous spaniel and a German shepherd the size of a pony.

Quite a few of the houses on Chelham Way and other streets in the vicinity had already been evacuated. At eleven forty-five the official order came from sound trucks going slowly up and down blaring out the message: **"This area must be evacuated. You have ten minutes to get out of this area. This area must be evacuated in ten minutes. You have ten minutes. . . ."**

It was enough. I grabbed a coat and three leashes. Ken put Brandy and Johnny in the back seat of the car and Rolls Royce in the front. Then he leaned down and kissed me and handed me the car keys. "Drive carefully."

"I thought you were coming with me."

"Drive carefully," he repeated. "And don't try to get in touch with me by phone. I'll be out on the ledge with a hose."

The sound truck went by again: **"This area must be evacuated immediately. You must leave now. This is your final warning."**

As I backed out of the driveway I saw Bertha Blomstrand climbing a ladder up to her roof. I called to her. She looked down at me and shook her head grimly. Her meaning was clear: everything she had worked for all her life was in that house and she wasn't going to abandon it.

She looked frail and impotent in the light of the fire that was now surrounding us on three sides, and the odds against her were formidable. Yet I know of dozens of houses that were saved in this manner—by one determined person with a garden hose—after the situation became so bad that firefighters and equipment couldn't be spared merely to save buildings, but had to be used for the much more important job of keeping the fire from spreading. **"This is your final warning."**

I joined the sad little procession of vehicles evacuating our street. Some had obviously been packed earlier in the evening. There was a pickup truck loaded with furniture and bedding held in place by two frightened children, a station wagon carrying suitcases and camping equipment, a tiny sports car jammed with Westmont College girls and their collections of photographs and folk-song albums and books. All I had was a coat and three leashes.

The Ferrys lived then as they do now on a knoll overlooking the Bird Refuge and the sea beyond. Ping was away on a business trip but Jo was waiting for me with her youngest daughter, Robin, a professional rider who'd driven up from the stables in Somis as soon as she heard about the fire. They both seemed calm, even cheerful, as though the glow in the sky and the pervasive smell of smoke were caused by nothing more than a Boy Scout marshmallow roast or a backyard barbecue. Zorba, the spaniel, represented the facts more accurately—he took one look at my dogs, barked nervously and fled to the rear of the house. Mine set off in pursuit and the game began that was to last, quite literally, all through the night.

Instead of making good use of the time by getting some rest, Jo and Robin and I sat in the library for a while and talked. Robin especially was to regret this since she was drafted to spend the next two nights helping look after some reluctant and difficult refugees at the polo field—150 show horses, mainly hunters and jumpers.

Eventually Jo showed me upstairs to my room, gave me a sleeping pill and said goodnight. There was a small radio beside the bed, and while I knew it would bring only bad news at this point, I couldn't resist turning it on. A man was announcing in a voice hoarse with fatigue that fifteen houses had been destroyed and a thousand men were battling the fire on a ten-mile front. There was no hope of containment so long as the santana kept blowing. Flames were fifty to seventy feet high and had already reached Cold Spring Canyon on the northeast, Gibraltar Road on the northwest, and Sycamore and Rattlesnake canyons on the west.

I turned off the radio and sat on the edge of the bed, the reporter's words echoing in my ears. I knew those canyons well and had spent many good hours birding in them, especially Rattlesnake Canyon, It was the topography, not the rattlesnakes, that had given the place its name, and the wildlife I encountered, except for deer and rabbits, and the occasional red fox and coyote, consisted mainly of birds.

At the old stone bridge that marked the canyon's mouth, hundreds of wintering robins and cedar waxwings fed voraciously on toyon and coffeeberries and the miniature apples of the manzanita. Oregon juncos and hermit thrushes bathed in the shallow pools. Bewick wrens picked their way fastidiously through the underbrush, pausing to catch a bug or denounce an intruder, and red-breasted sapsuckers played hide and seek with us around the trunks of the live oak trees. Wide-eyed kinglets rattled from leaf to leaf, every fidgety-twitchy movement distinguishing them from their look-alike but more phlegmatic cousins, the Hutton vireos, which were found in the same area though less frequently. The difference between the two species became unmistakable when two male kinglets met and the top of each tiny head burst into a crimson rage.

When spring came to the canyon, shooting stars, owl's clover, blue-eyed grass and milk maids bloomed in the sun, and in the shadier places, siesta flowers and Indian pinks, woodmint and the little green replicas of artists' palettes that are called miner's lettuce because the forty-niners used them for salads. It was then that the phainopeplas arrived to nest in the mistletoe, the lazuli buntings in the silver-lined mugwort along the stream, the Wilson warblers under the blackberry vines, the black-chinned hummingbirds in the sycamores, the cliff swallows under the stone bridge already occupied by a pair of black phoebes, the olive-sided fly-catchers in the pines, and Hutton vireos in the oaks, the western wood pewees and Bullock orioles in almost any tree or bush.

No summer rains fed the creek and by September some parts of it had turned to mud and some to dust, and the slow trickle of water was only a reminder of the past winter and a promise of the one to come. Along the banks the leaves of the poison oak turned orange and red, and its smooth white berries were eaten by wren-tits and California thrashers. Audubon warblers were everywhere, from the tops of the tallest trees where they flew out after insects like flycatchers, to the ground where they foraged like buntings. From ceanothus and chamise came the golden-crowned sparrows' sweet pleadings, "Hear me! Dear, hear me!" Pine siskins and American goldfinches gorged on the ripening seeds of the sycamores and alders, and high in the sky, white-throated swifts tumbled and turned and twisted with such speed that no single bird could be followed with the binoculars. (W.L. Dawson, in *Birds of California*, estimated that a white-throated swift which lives for eight years covers a distance equal to ten round trips to the moon.) Among the fallen leaves brown towhees foraged, both feet at a time, sounding like a whole battalion of birds, while tiny gray gnatcatchers searched the limbs of the pepper trees for grubs, and bushtits bickered through the oaks, followed by other little birds attracted by their antics and gay gossip—Townsend and Audubon and orange-crowned warblers, plain titmice and Hutton vireos, and in some years, mountain chickadees and red-breasted nuthatches.

This was Rattlesnake Canyon. I thought of all the small confiding creatures who lived in it and I wept.

The sleeping pill Jo Ferry had given me hit me very suddenly. I don't know what it contained but I can vouch for its effectiveness: I slept through the arrival and bedding down of my fellow refugees, a family of eleven with all their household pets, including a snake and a parakeet.

I woke up at dawn and became immediately aware of a change in the atmosphere. It was cold. The air coming in through the window was gray not with smoke but with fog, and it smelled of the sea, of kelp and tar and wet pilings. The santana had stopped.

I put on my coat, picked up the three leashes and made my way through the quiet house to the driveway, Zorba, the Ferrys' spaniel, was stretched out, dead to the world, under an olive tree. My three dogs were arranged around the car, panting even in their sleep, as though this was merely a short recess in a long game. At the sound of my step they were instantly alert and eager to go home. They hadn't the slightest doubt that there was still a home for them to go to. Their only anxiety seemed to be that they might have to be separated from me, so they all insisted on riding in the front seat. It was a cozy trip.

At the top of Barker Pass there was an abrupt change in the weather. The fog dropped away like a curtain and the air was hot and dry and windless and ashes were falling everywhere, some particles as fine as dust, some large as saucers. On Sycamore Canyon Road I came across a roadblock, but after a brief exchange of words I was allowed through. The men in charge looked too tired to argue. They had been up all night like hundred of other volunteer workers—students from the university and from City and Westmont colleges, Red Cross and Salvation Army workers, civil defense and National Guard units, radio hams, firemen's wives manning the stations while their husbands fought on the front lines, nurses and nurses' aide, teachers, city and county employees, and such a varied assortment as the members of a teen-age hot-rod club, a folk-dancing group, and a contingent of deep-sea divers from one of the offshore oil rigs.

I turned into Chelham Way.

It was like the fringe of a bombed area. The houses were still standing but deserted. In one driveway a late-model sedan was parked with a small U-haul trailer attached to the rear bumper. The trailer, heaped with clothes and bedding, had been left unprotected and the top layer of stuff was black with ashes. The sedan, however, was carefully covered with a tarpaulin. Perhaps its owner was a veteran of the disastrous 1955 Refugio fire, when a great many of us learned that ashes falling through atmospheric moisture made a lime mixture which ruined even the toughest paint.

Halfway around Chelham Way was a narrow black-top road leading to Westmont College. A locked gate kept the road unused except in emergencies. Beyond the gate, which was opened, I could see a large section of the athletic field where the main firecamp had been set up the previous day. Here, where Ken and I used to walk our dogs, where we watched robins in winter and track meets in spring, this place meant for nothing more than games was now headquarters for hundreds of men, a kind of instant village. Here they ate at canteen tents, slept on the ground, received first aid for burns and cuts, were sent off in helicopters, fire trucks, buses, pickups, jeeps, and brought back to begin the cycle all over again. The noise was deafening, most of it caused by the arrival and departure of helicopters and the shriek of sirens and blaze of loudspeakers. The "helitack" units of the Forest Service consisted of the pilots themselves, the fire jumpers wearing heavy canvas suits to protect them when they leaped into the bush, and ground crews, in orange shirts and helmets, whose job was to prime and space the copters and keep them out of each other's downdraft.

The scene, with its backdrop of blazing mountains, was unreal to me. Even the wounded men being brought in by helicopter looked like extras from the Warner Brothers backlot and the sirens of the ambulances as they left the field seemed like part of a sound track. The dogs knew better. They began to whine, so I let them out of the car and told them to go and find Ken. They didn't hesitate. It was a good place to get away from.

Beyond the road leading into the firecamp was the top of our canyon. This part, which belonged to Westmont College and had no structures on it, had been completely burned. The ancient oak trees were black skeletons rising from gray ashes, and many eucalyptus, cypresses and Monterey pines had been reduced to stumps, some still smoldering. But where the row of houses began, along each side of the canyon, the burning had terminated. There was no evidence that the area had been wetted down nor any reddish stains indicating the use of fire retardant; no firebreak had been bulldozed and no hose laid. Yet at that one particular point the fire had stopped.

I learned later what had happened. At two-thirty in the morning, just when all hope of saving our canyon had been abandoned, the santana ceased as abruptly as it began and the wind pressed in from the sea, cool and moist. Temperatures dropped, humidity rose, and the flames were pushed back toward the mountains. It was during this lull that the Los Angeles *Herald Examiner* went to press with the front-page headlines "SANTA BARBARA SAFE. FIRE SHIFTS: 18 HOMES LOST." By the time I got to read those headlines Santa Barbara was surrounded on three sides by an inferno and a hundred more houses had been lost.

I stopped the car. Through the binoculars I kept in the glove compartment I examined hollows where smoke was still rising and stumps still smoldering unattended. At any moment they could burst into flames

124

again and the santana could return. It had taken a miracle to save our canyon and there was probably only one to a customer. I rushed home to call the fire department.

Ken was asleep on the living-room davenport, a scribbled note on the coffee table beside him instructing me to wake him up when necessary. He didn't stir even under the barrage of dog greetings.

Most of the telephones in the region were out of commission by this time. Ours was still working, though it failed to solve much. The fire department, I was told, had no trucks and no men available; people spotting areas which were still smoking were urged to cover them with dirt and/or douse them with water. I grabbed a shovel and a length of garden hose and headed back up the road.

During the windless morning the fire went through a semi-quiescent phase. There was unofficial talk of "early containment," and a few evacuees began returning. Though the area where I was working still smoldered in places, other people had arrived to assist and the general picture looked good. By noon I felt secure enough to go home for some lunch. The only wildlife I'd seen all morning was an indignant family of acorn woodpeckers living in a nearby telephone pole, and a badly frightened and half-singed fox who came scurrying up from the bottom of the canyon.

Over tea and sandwiches Ken told me how he'd spent the night dousing sparks and embers that fell on the roof and in the underbrush. He had done his job well. Too well. The tea tree's natural tendency to lean had been encouraged by the excessive water and it now lay on its side on the ground. Many trees were lost to fire during that week; our tea tree was probably the only one lost to flood.

We were finishing lunch when my sister called to tell us the fire had started in another rampage. By midafternoon the "early containment" theory had been blown sky high—and sky high turned out to be the precise description. The flames jumped El Camino Cielo, the sky road, and were racing down the other side of the ridge, with nothing whatever

125

to stop them. Ten borate bombers were in operation, but dense smoke and wind conditions had grounded all of them and the fire roared unchecked into the back country, Santa Barbara's vulnerable watershed.

El Camino Cielo was the road along the top of the first main ridge, starting at the east end of Montecito and continuing west past the city of Santa Barbara, San Marcos Pass, Santa Ynez Peak, its highest point at 4292 feet, and ending at Refugio Pass. Along this sky road, winter bird watchers were apt to see mountain species which seldom appeared in the city itself—a Clark nutcracker noisily prying loose the scales of a pine cone; a varied thrush standing in regal silence underneath a live oak, ignoring the raucous challenges of Stellar jays; golden-crowned kinglets and brown creepers, mountain chickadees and red-breasted nuthatches, and sometimes a large garrulous flock of those erratic wanderers, the piñon jays.

* * *

The second night of the fire came on. At seven-thirty the heavy winds which had been blowing all afternoon at the upper elevations reached the foothills, and many of us found out for the first time what the term "wildfire" really meant. The whole mountain range seemed to explode, and flames were suddenly roaring down toward the city itself, through San Roque Canyon, Laurel Canyon, Mission Canyon, where the Botanic Garden was situated, all the way to Romero Canyon at the northeast end of Montecito. Because of the winds and approaching darkness the borate bombers stopped operating, and by this time too there was a drastic drop in water pressure.

Mass evacuations began, with some motels and hotels offering free rooms, and moving companies volunteering trucks and vans . Many people were double evacuees who'd fled Sycamore and Cold Springs canyons the first night and were now forced to flee their places of refuge; and before the fire was over, there was even a small band of very tired and jittery triple evacuees.

126

Our Chelham Way situation, which had been fairly good all day, was suddenly ominous again as the fire turned back in our direction. I thought of the house on Mountain Drive that had been saved in the afternoon only to be burned to the ground at midnight and I wondered what similar ironies might be preparing for us.

Blessing counters and silver lining searchers found a plus in a negative: there were no sightseers. The noise from the firecamp, however, was incredible, a continuous roar of helicopters arriving and departing, the blaring of air to ground loudspeakers, the shrieking of ambulance and fire truck sirens. It was decibels rather than danger which strained my nerves to the breaking point and convinced Ken I'd be better off elsewhere.

Jo Ferry called to repeat her invitation of the previous night, but Ken decided that this time more constructive action was necessary than simply sending me off with the three dogs. He made arrangements with my brother-in-law, Clarence Schlagel, to bring his pickup truck over. After a series of delays caused by roadblocks Clarence arrived with the truck and we loaded it with our main valuables, manuscripts and books. We owned no art originals, no fine china or silver, no furs, and I wore my two pieces of jewelry, my wedding ring and my "lucky" bracelet which had been a present from our daughter, Linda, many years before. (Some people we knew, trapped in the fire by a sudden, violent change of wind, used their swimming pool as a depository for their silver, jewelry and furs, including a beaver jacket whose original owner wouldn't have minded at all.)

It was agreed that I would go to the Schlagels' house with the two smaller dogs, leaving Brandy with Ken. That way Ken could rest at intervals during the night knowing that Brandy would wake him up if anything unusual happened. German shepherds have a highly developed sense of propriety and when things go wrong they indicate their disapproval readily and unmistakably. Having Brandy in the room was like having an alarm clock set to go off in any emergency. I rode in the truck with Johnny sitting quietly beside me and Rolls on my lap, trembling and whining all the way, partly out of fear and partly anticipation of spending another night chasing around the Ferrys' house with Zorba. He was in for a disappointment; no chasing was allowed at the Schlagels' place because there were too many chasers and chasees, and to avoid a complete shambles the animals had to be kept separated as much as possible. I counted four cats—a fat, ill-tempered orange tiger bought for Jane when she was a baby, an alley cat who realized he'd struck it rich and seldom left the davenport except to eat, and a pair of tabbies abandoned by a neighbor who'd moved away; Jane's pygmy poodle with the giant name of Cha Cha José Morning Glory, my sister's burro, Bobo, who had a loud, nervous hyena-type laugh he seemed to reserve especially for me, and Clarence's four Shetland ponies. Sibling rivalry was rather intense on occasion, and the arrival of Johnny who loathed cats, and Rolls who hated horses and rapidly learned to hate burros, didn't improve matters. There were many times during the night when I would have welcomed the sound of helicopters and fire sirens to drown out some of the yelping, yowling, whinnying, barking, and above all, Bobo's wild bursts of laughter.

I woke up at dawn, leashed my two dogs and took them for a walk down the road toward the sea. When I faced that direction everything seemed quite normal. The light breeze smelled of salt and moist kelp. Mourning doves and brown towhees foraged along the sides of the road and bandtails gathered in the eucalyptus trees, brown-headed cowbirds were already heading for the Schlagels' corral, Anna's hummingbirds hurled themselves in and out of fuschia blossoms and the bright red bushes of callistemon and torches of aloe, while half a dozen dogs vehemently denounced me and the company I kept.

When I turned to go back, the whole picture changed abruptly. I remember thinking, with terrible surprise as if I hadn't been aware of it before, **Our mountains are on fire, our forest is burning.**

Returning to the house, I found my sister and brother-in-law in the kitchen making breakfast and listening to the radio. It had been a disastrous night. With winds in forty-five mile an hour gusts and flames towering as high as two hundred feet, the firefighters didn't have a chance. Twenty-three thousand acres and over a hundred buildings were now destroyed and still the fire roared on, unchecked.

128

Fire. like war, is no respecter of age. Lost hysterical children wandered helplessly around Montecito village, and Wood Glen Hall, a home for the elderly at the opposite end of the fire area, was evacuated when the building filled with smoke.

Fire operates without any rules of fair play. Carol Davis of the University of California at Santa Barbara was helping the residents of Wood Glen Hall carry out their possessions when she learned that her own house had been destroyed and the only things saved were four books and few pieces of clothing.

Fire makes no religious distinctions. The Catholic Sisters of Charity were burned out, the Episcopalian retreat on Mount Calvary lost a building, and a residence hall was destroyed at the Baptist Westmont College.

Fire has no regard for history or politics. Several buildings were burned to the ground at San Ysidro Ranch, the site of one of the old adobes constructed when Santa Barbara was under Mexican rule, and the place where, in 1953, a young Massachusetts senator named Kennedy brought his new bride, Jacqueline Lee Bouvier, on their honeymoon.

Fire does not defer to beauty, either natural or man-made. A multi-million-dollar art collection belonging to Avery Brundage was destroyed, and some parts of the Botanic Garden were ravaged, including the majestic grove of sequoias, the largest of trees, where in the winter we could always find the tiniest of warblers, Townsend's, and in the spring the almost as tiny Oregon juncos nested under the fragrant heart-shaped leaves of wild ginger.

Even the firecamp itself wasn't spared. Flying embers started a blaze right in the middle of it and burned an area the size of a city lot before it was extinguished.

Around Santa Barbara that morning few people had a good word to say for Prometheus.

Ken phoned while I was feeding the dogs to tell us that he and Brandy and the house had come through the night in fair shape. Once again the flames had reached the head of our canyon and turned back as the winds shifted and though live coals had left holes in some roofs and all exterior areas were a mess, not a house on Chelham Way had been lost.

Other people weren't so lucky. Of my fellow refugees at the Ferrys' house, two were completely burned out: Robert M. Hutchins who lived in Romero Canyon in Montecito, and Hallock Hoffman who lived miles in the opposite direction above the Botanic Garden.

Every disaster has its share of ironies. Perhaps the Coyote fire seemed to have more simply because they happened to people we knew. One of them involved an old wooden shed which was on the Romero Canyon property where the Hutchins had built their house several years before. The shed was being used to store the antiques Mrs. Hutchins had been gathering from various parts of the world for her art shop. When it became inevitable that fire was going to overrun the area, the antiques were removed by truck and taken to—where else?—the Ferrys' house. No collector of irony will be surprised to learn that the old shed, highly inflammable, and containing nothing whatever of value, was the only building in the area untouched by flame.

One of the most eloquent of all the pictures taken during and after the Coyote fire was a shot of the formal gardens of the Brundage estate. It showed a marble Athena looking coolly and imperturbably through the bare black bones of trees toward the ruined mountains. No caption was needed; *Ars longa, vita brevis.*

* * *

It was still very early in the morning when I arrived home. For us the fire which had threatened on three sides was over. For others it was just starting. By noon 23,000 acres had burned, more than 2000 men were on the front and preparations were being made to start the backfire that was really to backfire and cause the first death.

Our house and yard, in spite of a covering of gray ash, looked beautiful to me because they were still there.

*Michael Collins is the pseudonym used by Edgar Award-winning Santa
Barbara writer Dennis Lynds (b. 1924) for his Dan Fortune detective
novels, including* Castrato *from which the following excerpt comes.*

THE CAR THAT CUTS YOU OFF

THE CAR THAT CUTS YOU OFF is always a
Mercedes. Or a pickup truck. The shiny car that turns from
a side road and forces you to slam on your brakes as it drives
on oblivious is a Mercedes or Jaguar or Rolls Royce. Or a pickup truck
with a lone male at the wheel. It is a Mercedes that parks in no-parking
zones, drives the wrong way against the arrows in a parking lot.

She is at the window table facing the lawn and Channel Drive in the
alcove of the cocktail lounge of The Biltmore. It is winter, the islands are
clear far out over the water. There are a lot of Mercedes and Jaguars and
even a few Rolls Royces on Channel Drive and in the hotel parking lot.

She drinks a Corona. Lee thinks it amusing that a woman as young as
she drinks beer. He calls her his cheap date, kisses her when he says it,
squeezes her hand. He is late. She knew he would be. She parked out on
Channel Drive to avoid the young Latino attendants who stare at her,
crossed the elegant hotel lobby alone. She is always aware of the faint
reaction, the heads that turn, the half step of the bell captain before he
notices her clothes, the briefcase. Less than the reaction of the lawyers,
the judge, the court attendants, her first day in court. Less than each time
she rises before a new judge or courtroom. Much is relative. The not-too-
important. The really important isn't relative. There are absolutes.

Lee is always late. She is sure it is a matter of status. Status and im-
portance. The man who must wait loses face. With women it doesn't re-
ally matter, but habit is hard to break. He will have a reason, an explana-

tion, as he kisses her and sits and looks immediately for the waitress. A late hitch in a deal. A meeting with an official—state, county, city—for some vital aid to get into or out of something. A call from his lawyer.

She orders another beer. She doesn't really expect him to care that much, knows by now what she is to him and what she can never be, but she wants to have her say and needs to relax. The Anglo cocktail waitress radiates more hostility than lobby or courtroom. Probably thinks she is a hooker plying her trade in the waitress's domain. Again, there is progress. Thirty years ago the waitress would have been sure a young Latina drinking alone in The Biltmore was a hooker and ordered her out. Fifty years ago she wouldn't have been allowed in the front door of The Biltmore. A hundred years ago the only relation she could have had with the Cantons was to wash their clothes. Or, of course, the one she has with Lee.

She is twenty-five years old, newly admitted to the bar and the list of *abogados* at La Casa, when she meets Tomas Lopez Villareal, a sixteen-year-old from Mexico. In the country a year. Illegal. He speaks no English, his Spanish isn't that good.

"The man he does not pay me. I work ten months, he pay me three-hundred-and-fifty dollar. Even the Lord's day I work. All day while the sun it is up. I ask that he will pay me, he say he tell *La Migra*."

The farm is on the vast Double C Ranch north of Los Alamos. Lopez has a dirty one-page letter in Spanish signed by Morgan Canton that agrees to pay $2.50 an hour. His actual pay has been nine cents an hour. He lives in an 8-foot-by-8-foot shed with a stove but no heat or running water. He is sometimes given a sack of beans and a package of tortillas. They check his story, take pictures, contact California Rural Legal Assistance. Together, they plan a lawsuit for back pay of $7175, plus $200,000 punitive and other damages arising from intentionally inflicted emotional distress and violations of California labor codes. Unless the Cantons will make full restitution out of court. She gets the case, CRLA makes an appointment for her to meet Morgan Canton.

She drives out in the new Honda Civic her father gave her when she passed the bar exam. The turnoff is hard to find, marked simply with a small intertwined pair of "Cs" and the name: Canton. The road is narrow, but blacktopped. A half mile into the brown hills she passes under a rustic arch with the Double C brand displayed much more proudly. A dirt track gouged by horses now runs beside the blacktop, like two centuries joined. It goes on and on for miles. At the first view of the sea she has to stop, get out to look at the sweep of brown oats and dusty green oaks and the shining ocean out to the distant islands.

"Hey! Hey!"

He is a teenager on a big brown horse with a silver-trimmed saddle. He wears the jeans, denim shirts, Western boots, wide-brimmed straw hat she has seen on all the farm boys in the state, but this boy has a fancy leather vest, spurs, and a real horse.

"You made a wrong turn five miles back, Miss. This is a private ranch."

"You work here?"

"I own the place." The boy smiles from the big horse. "I will. Me and Sam. My Dad and Granddad own it now. We been here over a hundred years. Built the whole place from scratch."

He isn't boasting, he is proud of what his name has built.

"Which one is Morgan?" she asks.

"That's me and my dad. If you come to see Dad, he's up at the house. Another five miles."

It sits down among the brown hills, sheltered, yet with a wide view of the sea and the islands. A real California ranch house. Parts of it true adobe, all of it whitewashed and dark-beamed and red-tile roofed. Corrals and barns and stables and fences. A large garage. Many horses and two Mercedes are visible. The boy has reached the house across country ahead of her, and a solid man of fifty-odd in the same jeans and denim shirt and leather vest and boots, but with a gray Stetson instead of the straw, stands with him on the veranda.

"Mr. Morgan Canton?"

"Do I know you, Miss?"

"Connie Ochoa. I have an appointment."

Morgan Canton has wind- and sun-creased eyes, a leathery face that is genuinely confused. He knows he isn't a man who forgets appointments, but...?

"Rural Legal Assistance called you. I'm an attorney."

"The boy says, "Uh-oh."

His father looks at him, and the boy misunderstands.

"Hey, how could I know? I means she's . . . I mean—"

"Do something, Morg," Morgan Canton says, and says to her, "I told your man it would be easier to talk to our lawyers in town."

"We thought if we spoke to you directly, we might settle the matter without any legal trouble or expense."

"What matter?"

She tells him Tomas Lopez Villareal's story, the investigation, the planned lawsuit.

"Hey," the boy cries. It is his expression for everything. "The *cholo's* a liar! We don't do stuff like that."

She and Morgan Canton both ignore the boy.

"If there is some mistake, Mr. Canton, a misunderstanding, I'm sure we can agree on proper restitution for Lopez."

"I'll look into it."

"Time is of the essence, Mr. Morgan. We'll have to file the suit if we don't hear from you soon."

"We'll look into it, Counsellor."

She drives the narrow ranch road back. The boy trails her on his horse, angry at the insult to the Cantons. A Mercedes appears behind her. It catches up and honks. She stops. A man gets out, strides up to her window. He is a younger, thinner version of Morgan Canton, perhaps forty.

"I'm Lee Canton. I was in the house. Want to talk?"

"I'm sure your brother—"

"Won't talk to me. I'm the black sheep, don't even live here. Maybe I can help. Its Attorney Ochoa, right?"

"Connie," she says. He acts more like an older Morgan the Third than a younger Morgan the Second.

"Lee. Let's go over to Mattei's Tavern."

It's been a long day, she is tense, and a drink sounds good. She follows Lee Canton's Mercedes to the old stagecoach station. They take a corner table in the empty afternoon bar where he seems well known. He has bourbon. She orders a Corona.

"You don't have to order beer," he says. "It's on me."

"I drink beer."

"Really? I never knew a young woman who drank beer. Is it something Mexican? I mean, a custom?"

She laughs. At last. "What did you want to talk about, Lee?"

"You mean besides getting your address and phone number?"

"Besides that."

"I didn't hear all of what you and Morg were saying."

She summarizes the charges of Tomas Lopez Villareal, and the lawsuit. Lee sips at his bourbon. His eyes are bright as if he is enjoying it all.

"You have pictures of the shed, the farm?"

"And the boy's pay records. Scraps of paper and money order receipts, but they look honest and we can't find any other cash."

"What did Morg have to say?"

"That he'd look into it."

He is, she realizes, excited. She senses that he is a soft man compared to his brother. This is why she thought of him as more like his young nephew. He is the different Canton, perhaps weaker, less sure of himself, less confident, but more human.

"He'll look into what my old man wants him to do, that's what he'll look into. That's why I got out years ago."

"You don't get along with your father?"

"The second son, right?" He waves for another round. "Morg does everything Sam's way, I do everything wrong. Standard Psych 101. When I tried to be a rancher, sit tall in the saddle, I blew it. He gave me a rundown construction company he'd been stuck with, told me if I could run it it was mine. I still run it, and a lot more. We can't all be ramrod night herders."

She'd had enough Psych 101 herself to know his father means more to him than he pretends. It makes him even more human. Her mother isn't really happy with a female lawyer. A Latin woman must not make men feel less.

"How old is he, your father?"

"Seventy-five this year. Born in the last century. Don't let that fool you. If he fights, he won't be easy to beat. I'll do what I can, Morg at least listens to me sometimes."

"What can he do? We have the boy's statement, the contract, the photos."

He twirls his glass. "Last year Morg caught young Morgan snorting C. He grabbed the kid's supplier, beat the shit out of him, and hauled him to the sheriff's office in Santa Maria. The bleeding hearts demanded the DA charge Morg with vigilantism, kidnapping, assault. The twenty-year-old pusher sued for $150,000 damages." He drinks. "Morg paid a fine for disorderly conduct. The kid pusher was arrested, took a plea to possession and a suspended sentence, settled out of court, and moved away."

"I see."

"One lawsuit Sam doesn't fight could lead to fifty more. He can make it hard to win, hard on you, and hard on that boy."

"But you'd help us fight him?"

"For you, I'll fight dragons."

They both laugh, have a third round. She agrees to see him again. He is married, but separated from his second wife. They talk about the Lopez case. One thing leads to another. He has never had a Latina, finds her exotic, exciting. She likes that, likes being with a man she can talk to about what she never can with Latin men she knows in Santa Barbara. She likes the crossing of so many barriers, the differences in them, that he so obviously finds her fascinating as a woman.

It turns out that a foreman on the Canton Ranch is the one cheating Tomas Lopez and other illegal field laborers. The Cantons say they will fire him, offer to give the boy his back pay but nothing more. The lawsuit is filed. The Canton lawyers counterfile for various delays, motions, exceptions, dismissals, and denials. The case drags on. She sees a lot of Lee Canton. He is nice, but can't do much to help against his father and brother. It is a long summer.

In late fall, Morgan Canton calls and summons her to the ranch to discuss the case.

"My father wants to see you."

The office in the old ranch house in relatively small, full of leather, old wood, books, ledgers, photographs as old as the wood, paintings of cowboys. Cluttered and comfortable. For a time she thinks that to see her is exactly what Sam Canton wants and nothing more. After his initial greeting, "Sit down," he sits in his desk chair and swivels slowly from side to side as if he were on a walking horse, and studies her.

He is smaller than both his sons, but thick and solid like Morgan. Darker skinned. His face is broader, almost Indian, his mustache thick and dark, his hair iron gray. His hands are small, and the skin is not wrinkled but soft like pale glove leather. He looks many years younger than seventy-five, except for his eyes. They are light brown flecked with green, and there is a hundred years of owning the land behind them.

"You're Mexican."

"No," he says, "I'm American."

He swivels. She notices the chair makes no sound. It is well oiled. Sam Canton takes care of details.

"My mother was Mexican. She was proud of it. Fine people, the Mexicans. Good friends, tough enemies. My mother was proud of her people."

"Were her people proud of her, Mr. Canton?"

He continues to swivel, as if he has spent so much of his life on a horse he can't think or talk without being in motion.

"She had her family, Miss Ochoa. Descended on both sides from the soldiers that came with Portola, three *commandantes* of the royal Presidio, one governor of Alta California. Her father owned ten times this ranch. It took my father five years to get the old don to let him marry my mother, another five to get this land as dowry. The old don didn't give anything away easily."

"But your father got the land."

"He got the land."

"And all the people on it, and around it, and hired by it? The Mexican people who weren't part of your mother's family."

The slow swivelling has a soothing, lulling effect in the small office.

"He got the land, and I got it, and Morgan will get it, and young Morgan and young Sam after that."

"Not Lee?"

For the briefest of seconds she sees a flicker in his eyes, amusement, and realizes he knows all about her and Lee.

"Lee doesn't count."

"Because he doesn't do what you want? Does everyone have to do what you want, Mr. Canton? Lee, the Lopez boy, the sheriff, the California Rural Legal Assistance, Casa de la Raza, me?"

Even as she says it she knows that she is missing the point. That what Sam Canton himself wants is not important. It is something else, and he isn't thinking about what she has said.

'You're a woman. A Mexican woman. A good-looking woman. I'm an old man, but I can appreciate that. I'll always admire a good-looking woman. I'll always appreciate a really pretty *chicana* like you."

She feels her anger, and at the same instant realizes that he is making her say what she is going to say. He is making the meeting go where he wants it to go.

"I'm a lawyer, Mr. Canton. I'm here as a lawyer."

"That's what's giving me some trouble, Miss Ochoa. I'm not sure how to deal with it. It's a big change. I don't know if it's a good change. It comes from different values, different ideas. I think it's going to destroy the country as I know it, as it has to be for a man like me." He is making a speech—one he has led her into so he can tell her something he wants her to know. "I told you about my mother and her ancestors. Ancestors and descendants, Miss Ochoa. Family. Everyone has a place. My mother's father got the land, my father developed it. The women had the children to continue it, protect it. A man builds, a woman continues. A man builds for himself and his family. The strong survive and pass it on."

138

The silence of the small office, study, whatever it is, is total. No sound of the moving chair. Not even a distant dog.

"The ranch is what counts," she says. "Your family is the world."

"Then you'll understand when I talk to you as a lawyer and only a lawyer. When I tell you we'll fight your lawsuit as long and as hard as necessary. We will give no cooperation. The foreman is gone, the incident is closed. It was our problem, we have solved it. We will not let you, or your organization, or the state of California, or anyone or anything decide what this ranch should do."

She walks out into the sun and brown hills and wide view of the sea and gets into her car and drives back to Santa Barbara. No one follows her this time. At the Casa she learns that Tomas Lopez Villareal has returned to Mexico. "Fifty thousand dollars," her boss says. "He can support his mother and sisters for twenty years in Oaxaca. They saved a bundle, but that wasn't what counts."

"No," she says.

The Casa and Rural Legal Assistance drop the lawsuit.

In the empty cocktail lounge she wonders if she went on seeing Lee to get back at the old man, the way Lee took up with her in the first place as a defiance of Sam Canton.

She won't be unfair. Lee genuinely likes her as a woman, if not the kind of woman he is used to, and there is the titillation of sex with a lawyer, the hint of taboo with a Latina. There is the divorce, and he is a man who has to have a woman.

(He married his first wife in San Francisco on a last foray at living and working outside Santa Barbara. The job lasted one year, the apartment two, the wife three. He is not a man who can live alone. The job and the apartment didn't send him home, but the wife did. No one knows where she disappeared to, she never wrote. He speaks of it now as a clean break, mentions her name, Janet, fondly, and implies that the end was a mutual blessing.

Two years later, installed at the construction company, he married the daughter of a local tycoon. This marriage was stormy from the start.

Extravagance, infidelities, bankruptcies, no children. It lasted fifteen years, neither husband nor wife ready to give up the advantages, and privileges of being a Canton and a Waite for the hazards of single life, or a new, perhaps lesser, attachment. So it lasted until just before she, Connie Ochoa, *abogado*, arrived on the scene.)

His Mercedes turns in for the valet parking. She waits for him to reach the table, kiss her, wave for the waitress.

"God, what a day."

"Business or personal?"

He orders his bourbon and her Corona. He hears the tone of her question that isn't a question. But, as usual, he hears it only through his preconceptions.

"Hey, we're in a bad mood."

"Finish your drink, Lee."

That is the ritual. The first drink is taken deep and long, the reward of a busy day.

"Ahhhh."

The bourbon is gone—before the ice can kill it. The joke is part of the country club bar scene when the bosses gather for one or two before they go home to their wives. This time he doesn't say it. He senses she has something on her mind, only motions for another drink.

"A young man came to my office last week." She shakes her head to the waitress. Three beers are enough. "Single, been in town for ten years. He's got a good job, wants to buy a home, hasn't enough cash for a down payment. He heard about the 'affordable' home program, found he qualified."

"Lucky him."

"He went to the county, they sent him to a condo developer. The developer says the 'affordable' units will be given out by lottery. Two weeks later he hears the units are all sold, calls county and developer. The county says the units can't be sold, they must approve any sale. The developer says the lottery will be soon. Another two weeks, same story. The young man goes to the development. People are being shown units, he asks a saleswoman about the 'affordables.' She is curt, they are all sold. Now he's really mad, goes back to county and developer. All is well, he will be contacted." She twirls her empty bottle. "One more week. He calls the developer. The units are sold. It's over. The end. So he comes to me."

"What can you do? Developers don't have to hold a lottery."

"I can find out what happened to those 'affordables' all you developers have to build for the young and the old, the poor and the disadvantaged, to get city approval for any development."

He laughs.

"All five units were given to 'friends' of the developer before a nail was driven. All of them qualified, but none of them had shown interest in owning a condo before. I mean, I know most of them too, don't I? Since you're the developer."

He smiles, drinks. "It's all legal, Con. Nothing says how I have to sell the 'affordables' as long as the people qualify. The kid won't be so gullible next time. Hey, you want to help him? Give me his name, I'll see what I can do."

"That's not the point, Lee."

"Then what the hell is the point?"

"That you and your 'friends' will sell those 'affordables' at full market price and split the profits. That the young and the old, the poor and the disadvantaged are robbed again."

He calls for another bourbon.

"What's this all about, Con?"

She looks toward the waitress. "The waitress doesn't like me. She's right. A waitress needs lords and ladies to give her big tips, to be hood-winked and lived off. People like me will ruin her world."

"Am I supposed to understand that?"

'Your father would, but never mind. The deal with the affordables is just the tip of the iceberg, Lee. There's the Rolls Royce, the solar heating, the—"

"Hey, honey!" He grins at her, drinks the bourbon too fast. "The Rolls was all mixed up in the divorce. Okay, I shouldn't have tried to get money out of the insurance company, but the judge was going to give Pauline the car. When I had McElder hide it, everyone thought it had been stolen. I needed cash, I wasn't thinking straight. The judge believed me. I paid it all back."

"The solar heating, the earthquake repairs, the land deal?"

"There's nothing illegal about the solar heating. We sold those units in good faith, passed on what the manufacturers told us they'd do. It wasn't our fault the buyers didn't get the savings they expected, and we really thought their houses would increase in value. I'm not alone in that suit, there's thirty-five contractors and sixteen lenders, and they haven't ruled against us yet."

"Is it legal to tell mobile home owners a new state law requires stricter earthquake safety standards when there isn't any such law? Then hustle them into repairs they can't afford, get down payments bigger than the law says you can?"

"I only invested, Con. I didn't know what they were doing."

"You knew what you were doing when you faked that letter saying Fed-Mart wanted to buy land you were selling, got an inflated appraisal of the value. You'd have been charged if it hadn't fallen through and the buyer didn't want to look stupid."

He holds his drink, leans back. "What is all this, Connie?"

She glances around the elegant lounge. "Did you ever notice that when a car cuts you off it's always a Mercedes or a pickup?"

"You've lost me."

Now she wishes she had another beer, watches the waitress. "When the adventurers, the farm boys, the debtors got off the boat in America they immediately adopted the attitudes of the nobility. That's from a history book, but it's true and it hasn't changed All that mattered was their interest, their advantage, their power. Freedom meant to exploit, rob, cheat even kill to get for themselves and keep it. They still think the same, Lee, in more modern terms, and so do you."

He is silent for a time. "You're telling me we're through?"

"You're exactly like your father, Lee. The flip side of the record. Your father's principles without principles." A weak Sam Canton. Denial not confrontation. Cunning not strength. Coyote not eagle, but both predators. "Everything you do is to show your father he was wrong about you, but it won't work. Tricks and schemes don't impress Sam Canton. Strength does. Strength and power, and you don't have either and never will."

"Thank you , Miss Ochoa. Thank you very much."

"I can never be a serious woman for you, Lee. You're the marrying type, and you could never marry me. That would be defying your world, the country club, the powers that be."

It has taken her months to realize all she has said, but on his face she sees that he has understood in an instant. They are wrong for each other. She wants out. He is off the hook.

"What are you going to do, Con?"

His fatherly tone almost makes her laugh. She hails the waitress, orders another Corona and a bourbon for him. It's all right now.

"Put it on my check." She takes a tiny clipping from her bag. "Let me read you something, Lee. Dateline, Santa Ana 'A homeless woman has given the city $20 for her two-year use of public restrooms at Santiago Park. The note, signed Jane Lee, simply said, **I am a homeless person and have used Santiago Park for two years.** I'm going to work for people like that, Lee."

She feels totally relaxed. His smile is almost real.

"A newborn militant, Con?"

"A fighter for a new world."

"Government control? Socialism? You'll kill the country. My Dad, much as I'm *not* like him, is what made this country."

"You're right. Sam Canton *is* what made this country." She drinks."I think what most people want, Lee, is a varying number of needs and services, then to be left reasonably alone. Beyond that, I'd rather have a society where the rich are the criminals, not the poor. Where the arrogant are ignored, not the humble. Where the thoughtful and fair and brotherly are admired, not the pushy and powerful and rapacious."

""Well," he finishes his bourbon, looks at his watch, "I guess that leaves me out." He seems about to reach out and take her hand, stops.

"What do I say? It's been good? I'm sorry it came out like this? I am sorry. Can we stay friends?"

"I'll ask you that after we tangle a few times in court."

It isn't the answer he expected, and he will never know what to do with what he doesn't understand. He stands, drops money on the table.

"Have another beer, Con." He shakes his head. "Beer! That should have told me from the start we'd never make it."

He bends quickly, kisses her cheek.

She says, "Does your father drive a Mercedes or a pickup truck? No, don't tell me. He drives both, right?"

He smiles in total incomprehension before he walks from the lounge. Alone, she leans back in the chair, looks out at the wide lawn and Channel Drive and the sea and the islands beyond. She doesn't even notice the waitress when her beer comes.

Christopher Buckley (b. 1948), a widely published poet, grew up in Santa Barbara, attending Mt. Carmel and Bishop Garcia Diego High School. He taught at UCSB for five years in the English Department. This essay is from his recently published book, Cruising State: Growing up in Southern California.

FLAT SERVE

I T   W A S   N O T   D I V O R C E, nor business partners who stole him blind, nor the fortunes in real estate he should easily have made, nor the fact that he just missed fame as a singer with a big band; it was surfing, surfing broke my father's heart.

I was given my first tennis racket at age two and by four I was dragging it around between games in my father's Sunday matches on the parking lot-like court in Manning Park. This was '52 and the racket was squared-off, strung as loosely as a fish net with what they then called "cat gut." I would stand just inside the service line and hit balls lobbed toward me from across the net, and when I connected, my racket would slingshot the ball toward the blue, from where it finally sank to bounce high off the chicken wire fence. The racket was cheap and built for an adult; the grip was too thick, and so I often took a swing with both hands and was always quickly corrected on my form. And when I got caught smashing acorns on the cement picnic table with it, I received my first lecture on the correct use and care of rackets.

I was soon learning a proper forehand, and when I was able to remember to get to the courts after school, that is as early as six years old, my father began to hold forth on the moral imperative of a flat, power serve—Big Bill Tilden hit in that way, first and second serve, and so would

145

I. He praised Pancho Gonzales as well—a cannonball first server—but couldn't for the life of him figure out why Gonzales put spin on the second ball. And as far as I could tell there was something equally corrupt in a slice backhand; it was for "dinks" and "pushers" I soon learned. Don Budge was the master of the backhand drive and my father proclaimed the absolute virtue of a flat, one-handed stroke. Rosewall with his slice, Segura with his two-handed chip, why Budge would have killed them both! This was a matter of a character and I was going to have it.

Lucky for us both I had the talent that I did. The pro, Byron De Mott, said I was a natural; moreover at lessons, I hit the ball harder than anyone else and liked it—so my father seemed relieved if not happy. Weekends I was religiously at the courts. All through grammar school I got off the bus at day's end and walked up the road to the country club courts. I was growing up among the rich, in a rich fashion almost. For while my father was a DJ for a local station and mother worked as a secretary for the city schools, we lived on a full acre in Montecito, the woodsy section of town flanking the foothills. My parents built our house pretty much on their own, and across the street was a wilderness of scrub oak, acacias, laurel, and eucalyptus, even the out of place palm tree by a pool or creek. I knew the trails and the borders of ferns, the maroon shade or the air stunned with sunlight atop house-sized boulders which just sat outright on the land like worn idols from a chapter heading in Bible History. I took it all simply on faith; days passed as slowly as drifting clouds and were full of coveys of quail, wild peacocks, chipmunks, lizards, gliding spirals of hawks before the sandstone face of mountains. It was that simple. No choices had to be made, no judgments; there was nothing and everything to do under the sky. To be sure, there were large, private estates, manicured grounds, a fountain or two—a little old money here and there belonging to folks who had made it big in the market and moved here to beat the Chicago winters. Most mansions were back of the trees—long drives we could never sneak all the way up without being run off by a caretaker. Yet it seemed people could live anywhere they wanted. I had friends whose uniform cords had as many rips in the knees as mine, yet who lived in huge homes, ranch houses, two story haciendas with fruit trees and automatic sprinklers. I'd stay over night and we could climb in the avocado trees or run down their hills. It seemed perfectly natural to always be running though all that space.

But more and more I had less time for my friends. The pro at the club struck a deal for my father. Byron thought I was a prospect and for nothing more than the love of the game and out of his good nature, he talked whoever was in charge into allowing me to hang out at the courts and play so long as my father paid for one lesson a week. I spent all my time there without having to join the club, something we never could have afforded. And while adults could kick any kid off any court, I soon saw there was a difference among apparent equals. Most of the others, after putting in the required time at group lessons or seeing who could hit the most balls over the fence onto the fairways, spent their time racing down to the grill for hamburgers and shakes; they just signed their names on their parents' tab and came away with everything. Even when I went to pick up lunch for Byron and was encouraged to order an ice cream for myself, I never did. Something in the eyes of the waiters made me feel they knew I had no business ordering or signing for anything.

A couple of long summers hitting against the backboard had passed, and in local tournaments I was making the finals where I lost to Johnny Fitz or Benny Weiss, boys slightly older who'd been playing longer and had more lessons. My father dropped me off early in the mornings and came by after work, when everyone else had left. Johnny's father, Harley Fitz, was often at the club. I wondered what Harley did. When Johnny was playing, he coached through the fence, always trying to psyche-out Johnny's opponent. One day when I was serving well, I almost beat Johnny, and though he had seen me play before, Harley turned back toward the court as he and Johnny headed for the grill and said, "Stick around kid, we'll make a star out of you too." For a moment, I was flattered for the attention, but soon felt put down and resentful. I wondered if he had been talking to my father. But my father was rarely at the club and never went to the grill; I don't think he would have talked to Harley anyway. Harley

147

wore alligator shirts with a blue blazer and gray slacks, and cordovan loafers without socks, which I thought was very strange. He was always headed for the grill once Johnny had the match in hand, and toward the end would reappear—his face red, his thin hair white in contrast, and the sound of his voice commenting on the points. Among the women, there was Benny's mother who always arrived after lunch in her white, convertible Mercedes with a large white chow stationed in the front seat, Benny and his older brother in the back. Her hair was frosted, streaked with long lines of gold over the gray; her head seemed to match the many bracelets and necklaces which rattled about as she played doubles on the first court with Mattie De Mott—the golden blossoms of the eugenia hedge blooming, the omniscient sunlight, a whole bright world spangled in starched tennis whites. They played with a stiff gentility and displayed no desire to put the ball away, even if the ability had been there. I hated being kicked off the courts by people who couldn't hit it.

One day Byron wanted to teach me a slice serve. My father was not there and so I decided to give it a try, tossing the ball out to my right and hitting around it instead of over the top. There was a swishing "ping" sound like a dull harp being plucked, and fluff from the thick nap of the Dunlap ball suspended for a second in the air. It worked the first time, landing in the far forehand corner and abruptly jackknifing into the side fence for an ace. It was quite a trick for someone my age and I used it especially for the second serve, but I was pressured into hitting it flat for both serves when my father watched in tournaments, or when I went through a full shopping cart of practice serves after my weekly lessons. He paid for the racket, the lessons and my one set of tennis clothes. I had a Lacoste shirt and Jack Purcell shoes, the ones with the large half-dome of rubber over the toe, the heavy ones that lasted best. While more than once I wore my high-top P F Flyers until holes in the soles made holes in my socks, while the knees of my corduroys were layered with iron-on patches, I had the gear for tennis. He just knew I would make something of myself. And at thirteen I had my photo in *World Tennis* for winning some tournaments in Palm Springs and for him it looked like this might make up for something he'd missed out in the world.

148

That year I moved down the hill to the municipal courts. There were more and better programs for junior tennis, more competition and tournaments. But I suspected it was because Mike Koury, the pro there, gave weekend lessons for free, that I was told to ride my bike and play there instead of at the country club. Also by then, the club probably wanted us to pay up. I also think my father realized Byron had taught me the spin serve, or maybe he'd seen him hit a slice backhand, or, God forbid, his "Peruvian"—a trick shot that amazed kids and club players alike, from the forehand side he would hold the racket face-like plate, flat-up at the sky, then hit under the ball with a tremendous backspin, and the ball would hit on the other side of the net and draw back over before the opponent could reach it; definitely not stuff for future champions. I improved with Koury. He called me "bull-moose" and worked with me on the serve and volley game. There was always the pressure to win, to beat the boys from the club in tournaments, and I went through a temperamental streak, smashing a few rackets, throwing others into the podocarpus trees which lined the courts. But even when I outgrew that stage, I went through my Victor Imperial gut every two weeks; the combination of hitting the cannon-ball flat serve followed by the slicing can-openers and high-hopping American Twists was deadly for strings. Playing a power game mushed-out the wooden frames in a month, so it was a good thing I could earn my own rackets; I was able to garden around the nine courts and stadium earning a dollar an hour toward frames and strings at Koury's Pro Shop.

I began high school at a prep school, in Ojai, California, a small horsey town about an hour and a half south and inland from Santa Barbara. Football was the thing there, and so I felt compelled to play in the fall and winter instead of practicing full-time for tennis. But there was as much or more pressure to conform and produce according to a standard, and so when spring came I did not go out for training with the rest of the guys in crew cuts, but rather played on the tennis team. We had good players and won the tri-valley conference. Things looked good until the summer when I drew Bob Lutz in the first round of a big tournament and there wasn't much I could do. My serve won me five games in two sets which my friends assured me was a good showing. Later that month, playing in both the Thirteens and Fifteens, I was clobbered by a couple other hot players, my father remembering one of them as a young Stan Smith. Whoever they were, I kept things in perspective—those guys were from L.A. and already famous, especially Lutz. Overall, it still came pretty easily and I played for the Santa Barbara city team on weekend trips against Oxnard, Ventura, and Ojai, and at summer's end against the team from the L.A. Tennis Club. One year, Clayton Smith and I beat Hobson and Rombeau, two top-ranked players in the 16s, and that was really the last grand moment in tennis for me. They walked on to the courts in matching Jack Kramer creme colored whites, carrying about six or eight rackets apiece, joking to themselves about us like we'd just fallen off the last turnip truck from Bakersfield. Clayton had a Jack Kramer jacket and we both had two rackets, though they were different makes, which showed we weren't on any "free list" from a manufacturer like ranked players. Clayton poached well and put the ball away with crisp, angle-volleys; my serve and overhead were on. It took three sets for us to beat them, with Hobson changing rackets every couple games as if losing were a fault of his equipment. Santa Barbara lost the match but we felt great anyway. That was the second summer of prep school, but when my father could no longer pay the bill I was allowed to attend the local Catholic high in Santa Barbara, which was where I really wanted to be.

That was the end of the 50s and start of the 60s and next to nobody was surfing though Santa Barbara had several good spots as I would find out later. Then, only a few old guys in their thirties were in the water on planks and "big guns" in Hawaii, or south of town at Rincon Point. They were considered beatniks and no one thought much about it. But now a lot of my friends were surfing. Those were innocent days when you could leave your board strapped to racks on top of your '59 Chevy in the school parking lot and it would still be there when you got out of class. There were good beaches with lefts and rights and a swell always running, or so it seemed, especially in early fall when school began and September was hotter than any summer month. The last class would let out and there

150

would be an exodus for Hope Ranch, The Pit, Hammond's Reef, or Miramar Point.

Surfing meant social distinctions as well. It was easy acceptance as long as you really went into the water; everybody knew who the "hodads" were, those who dressed the part and drove their woodies to surf spots without ever taking their boards out of the back. And there was a dress code—white Levis, T-shirts, and wool Pendleton shirts. We all wore blue tennis shoes. If you were really cool you wore Sperrys, and if you weren't, the less popular Keds. But if you were a surfer it was blue. At the city Rec dances you would band together with other surfers mostly, but at school dances there was no need for group protection. Then there were the movies—for surfers they were the most important social event. Bruce Brown filled the vast Santa Barbara High auditorium time and again with *Surfing Hollow Days*. John Severson had a big hit with *Big Wednesday* featuring famous surfers Ricky Gregg and Greg Knoll out-racing twenty-five foot walls at Waimea or Makaha. In those days, two-to-four swells ran much of the summer and we were in the water as long as there was light. For weeks at a time we were happy and unbothered in our lives.

The tennis coach at Bishop High School was incompetent, a fact he tried to hide with an officious and authoritarian manner. I was the one player he could do without as I would expose the fact that he had no idea what he was doing. I was a threat. His condescending attitude and verbal cuts clearly conveyed that to me. I went out to the first two practices, hit some forehand and backhand drives past his ears and never showed up again. He lost the best player he could get, but was smug and happy about it. He then could work the other, mostly beginning players, without too much embarrassment to himself.

I took a part-time job at the local grocery chain and that paid for my car, a new board, and gas to go north or south looking for waves. On the Feast of Immaculate Conception or the Feast of the Assumption, we'd load our boards in a friend's VW bus by 5:30 and be pulling off the 101 Freeway as the sun came up, determined to get Rincon to ourselves while all the public-school guys wrestled with algebra or sweated out biology.

151

And on days I didn't want to drive that far, I hit Hope Ranch, a beach break with no rocks, where I sometimes ran into three or four friends I used to play singles or doubles with at the municipal courts. It was good to be a local and know people, then there was no fighting over the waves. We were all, in our rice-paddy baggies, civil to each other, and were concentrating on trying to ride the nose with that casual aplomb we'd seen Phil Edwards display in the films. Phil was the first one to ride the Banzai Pipe Line in Hawaii, the tubes streaming in overhead and breaking on a shallow bed of coral which accounted for the shape and power. We'd all seen Edwards crank a hard left bottom-turn, crouch about a foot from the nose and come flying out of the curl with the wave spitting spume close behind. Or at Malibu, on waist-high sections, there was Phil, nonchalant as you please, riding six inches from the nose, feet parallel, both hands clasped casually behind his back. Ultimately cool. We were all "stoked" and spent hours wiping out and "pearling" off our boards in attempted imitation. My father silently gave up on pushing the tennis. Since I was paying for all my own expenses, there seemed to be nothing he could do. He just offered his half despondent look when I began loading the car with my gear.

I was in the water at every opportunity until I went away to college at a small school in northern California. I played a little on the tennis team but the captain was obsessive, a real "come-on-guys" type and the school did not furnish rackets or clothes. We were given little more than gas money and greasy sandwiches and told to drive to some state university for a match. For the rest of college I took up golf and played on the team and with friends. But during graduate school, especially in summers, I was playing tennis again—largely out of economic necessity, as I could land jobs teaching at courts around town in the city's summer program. By summer's end I was usually playing even with friends who had been at it all year. Yet one kid I had beaten with regularity years before had become a celebrity of sorts, winning tournaments in Los Angeles and in the east. Word was he had just signed with Philadelphia for World Team Tennis. For me, well, it was just too late, though I could make it a couple rounds in local summer tournaments. My father knew this, though he hadn't seen me play since I was fourteen. Nevertheless, I was offered a job at one of the local clubs; my old pro, Mike Koury, seemed to be making the recommendation, and he put my name in based on my ability as a teacher I guess. It was then a choice between more school or a permanent job in the sun, playing the other local pros a couple times a week, watching the station wagons pull up summer mornings and the kids pour out like Myrmidons across the courts while the mothers went off for lunch on the terraces or patios beneath the blue shade of oak trees in Montecito. It was a choice between a life of writing or saying until I'm sixty something, "...better racket preparation Mrs. Johnson, bend the knees, left shoulder toward the net now, follow through all the way..."

Even though I wasn't going to make the WCT Tour, even though Bob Lutz had just spin-served and half-volleyed his way through the best players in the world to the U.S. Pro Indoor Title, even though his knees would begin to give out the next year and I'd never get another shot at him, my father was truly disappointed when I turned down the job. From that day forward, although I took my degrees, published and taught at universities, he would continue to sadly shake his head and tell anyone who would listen how surfing had ruined my career.

SANTANA CONDITIONS, UNIVERSITY BEACH

The soft warm wind is momentarily loud in the palm trees

I look out at the sea from the bluff, it is

in general a silver plaque fretted with black shadows

for the rest, a few dark zones, squalls—and a low surf

what I am hearing is a black sound of tangled
and cancelled low frequencies

with thematic displays in slightly higher registers
as the waves break at the shore in
bubbles of darkened silver

The blue sky with horn-like moon in its crown

is bordered by lush hazes of lemon yellow, orange, mauve

Edward Loomis
— *1972*

Sue Grafton (b. 1940) has continued the "Santa Teresa" mystery tradition with her best-selling alphabetical Kinsey Milhone novels. They are widely admired and, because of their local descriptions, a special delight to Santa Barbara readers.

THE GROOMER

SANTA TERESA IS A Southern California town of eighty thousand, artfully arranged between the Sierra Madres and the Pacific Ocean—a haven for the abject rich. The public buildings look like old Spanish missions, the private homes look like magazine illustrations, the palm trees are trimmed of unsightly brown fronds, and the marina is as perfect as a picture postcard with the blue-gray hills forming a backdrop and white boats bobbing in the sunlight. Most of the downtown area consists of two-and three-story structures of white stucco and red tile, with wide soft curves and trellises wound with gaudy maroon bougainvillea. Even the frame bungalows of the poor could hardly be called squalid.

Living with the climate in Santa Teresa is rather like functioning in a room with an overhead light fixture. The illumination is uniform—clear and bright enough—but the shadows are gone and there is a disturbing lack of dimension. The days are blanketed with sunlight. Often it is sixty-seven degrees and fair. The nights are consistently cool. Seasonally it does rain but the rest of the time, one day looks very much like the next and the constant, cloudless blue sky has a peculiar, disorienting effect, making it impossible to remember where one is in the year. Being in a building with no exterior windows gives the same impression: a subliminal suffocation, as though some, but not all, of the oxygen has been removed from the air.

I left my apartment at 9:00, heading north on Chapel. I stopped for gasoline, using the self-service pump and thinking as I always do, what a simple but absurd pleasure it is to be able to do that sort of thing myself. By the time I found K-9 Korners, it was 9:15. The discreet sign in the window indicated that the place opened for business at eight. The grooming establishment was attached to a veterinarian's office on State Street just where it made the big bend. The building was painted flamingo pink, one wing of it housing a wilderness supply store with a mummy bag hanging in the window and a dummy, in a camping outfit, staring blankly at a tent pole.

I pushed my way into K-9 Korners to the accompaniment of many barking dogs. Dogs and I do not get along. They inevitably stick their snouts right in my crotch, sometimes clamping themselves around my leg as though to do some kind of two-legged dance. On certain occasions, I have limped gamely along, dog affixed, their masters swatting at them ineffectually, saying "Hamlet, get down! What's the matter with you!?" It is hard to look such a dog in the face, and I prefer to keep my distance from the lot of them.

There was a glass showcase full of dog-care products, and many photographs of dogs and cats affixed to the wall. To my right was a half door, the upper portion opening into a small office with several grooming rooms adjoining. By peering around the doorjamb, I could spot several dogs in various stages of being done up. Most were shivering, their eyes rolling piteously. One was having a little red bow put in its topknot, right between its ears. On a worktable were some little brown lumps I thought I could recognize. The groomer, a woman, looked up at me.

"Can I help you?"

"The dog just stepped on that brown lump." I said.

She looked down at the table. "Oh Dashiell, not again. Excuse me a minute," she said. Dashiell remained on the table, trembling, while she grabbed for some paper towels, deftly scooping up Dashiell's little accident. She seemed pretty good-natured about it. She was in her mid-forties with large brown eyes and shoulder-length gray hair, which was pulled back and secured with a scarf. She wore a dark wine-colored smock and I could see that she was tall and slim.

"Are you Gwen?"

She glanced up with a quick smile. "Yes, that's right."

"I'm Kinsey Millhone. I'm a private investigator."

Gwen laughed. "Oh Lord, what's this all about?" She disposed of the paper towel and moved over to the half door and opened it. "Come on in. I'll be right back."

She lifted Dashiell from the table and carried him into a back room just off to the left. More dogs began to bark and I could hear a blower being turned off. The air in the place was dense with heat, scented with the smell of damp hair, and the odd combination of flea syrup and dog perfume. The brown linoleum tile floor was covered with assorted clippings, like a barber shop. In the adjoining room I could see a dog being bathed by a young girl who worked over an elevated bathtub. To my left several dogs, beribboned, were waiting in cages to be picked up. Another young woman was clipping a poodle on a second grooming table. She glanced at me with interest. Gwen returned with a little gray dog under her arm.

"This is Wuffles," she said, half clamping the dog's mouth shut. Wuffles gave her a few licks in the mouth. She pulled her head back, laughing, and made a face.

"I hope you don't mind if I finish this up. Have a seat," she said affably, indicating a metal stool nearby. I perched, wishing I didn't have to mention Laurence Fife's name. From what Charlie Scorsoni had told me it would rather spoil her good humor.

Gwen began to clip Wuffles's toenails, tucking the dog against her body to prevent sudden moves. "You're local, I assume," she said.

"Yes, I have an office downtown here," I said, pulling out my I.D. automatically. I held it toward her so she could read it. She gave it a glance, apparently accepting it without much suspicion or concern. It always amazes me when people take me on faith.

"I understand you used to be married to Laurence Fife," I ventured.

"Yes, that's right. Is this about him? He's been dead for years."

"I know. His case is being opened up again."

"Oh, *that's* interesting. By whom ?"

"Nikki. Who else?" I said. "The Homicide Department knows I'm looking into it and I have their cooperation, if that helps you any. Could you answer some questions for me?"

"All right," she said. Her tone was cautious but there was also a note of interest, as though she considered it a curious inquiry, but not necessarily bad.

"You don't sound that surprised," I said.

"Actually I am. I thought that was finished business."

"Well, I'm just starting to look into it and I may come up with a blank. We don't have to talk here if it's inconvenient. I don't like to interrupt your work."

"This is fine with me, as long as you don't mind watching me clip a few dogs. I really can't afford a time-out right now. We're loaded today. Hold on," she said. "Kathy, could you hand me that flea spray? I think we missed a few here."

The dark-haired groomer left the poodle long enough to reach up for the flea spray, which was passed over to Gwen. "That's Kathy, as you might have gathered," Gwen said. "The one up to her elbows in soapsuds is Jan."

Gwen began to spray Wuffles, turning her face away to avoid the fumes. "Sorry. Go ahead."

"How long were you married to Fife?"

"Thirteen years. We met in college, his third year, my first. I'd known him about six months I guess."

"Good years? Bad years?"

"Well I'm mellowing some on that," she said. "I used to think it was all a big waste but now I don't know. Did you know Laurence yourself?"

"I met him a couple of times," I said, "just superficially."

Gwen's look was wry. "He could be very charming if he wanted to, but at heart he was a real son of a bitch."

158

Kathy glanced over at Gwen and smiled. Gwen laughed. "These two have heard my version about a hundred times," she said by way of explanation. "Neither has ever been married so I tend to play devil's advocate. Anyway, in those days I was the dutiful wife, and I mean I played the part with a dedication few could match. I cooked elegant meals. I made lists. I cleaned the house. I raised the kids. I'm not saying I'm anything unique for that, except that I took it awfully to heart. I wore my hair up in this French roll, not a pin out of place, and I had these outfits to put on and take off, kind of like a Barbie doll." She stopped and laughed at the image of herself, pretending to pull a string from her neck. "Hello, I'm Gwen. I'm a good wife." she burbled in a kind of nasal parrot tone. Her manner was rather affectionate as though she, instead of Laurence, had died but was remembered fondly by dear friends. Part of the time she was looking at me, and part of the time she combed and clipped the dog on the table in front of her, but in any event her manner was friendly—hardly the bitter, withdrawn account I'd expected.

"When it was over, I was pretty angry—not so much at him as at myself for buying into the whole gig. I mean, don't get me wrong, I liked it at the time and it suited me fine, but there was also a form of sensory deprivation going on so that when the marriage blew up, I was totally unequipped to deal with the real world. He managed the money. He pulled the strings. He made the major decisions, especially where the kids were concerned. I bathed and dressed and fed them and he shaped their lives. I didn't realize it at the time because I was just running around anxious to please him, which was no easy task, but now that I look back on it, it was really fucked."

She glanced up at me to see if I'd react to the language, but I just smiled back.

"So now I sound like all the other women who came out of marriages in that era. You know, we're all faintly grumpy about it because we think we've been had."

"You said you'd mellowed some," I said. "How did that come about?"

"Six thousand dollars' worth of therapy," she said flatly.

I smiled. "What made the marriage blow?"

Her cheeks tinted slightly at that but her gaze remained just as frank. "I'd rather save that for later if you're really interested."

"Sure, fine," I said. "I didn't mean to interrupt anyway."

"Well. It wasn't all his fault," she said. "But it wasn't all mine either and he hosed me with that divorce. I'm telling you, I got beat up.

"How?"

"How many ways are there. I was scared and I was also naive. I wanted Laurence out of my life and I didn't care much what it cost. Except the kids. I fought him tooth and nail over them, but what can I tell you? I lost. I've never quite recovered from that."

I wanted to ask her about the grounds for the custody battle but I had the feeling it was touchy stuff. Better to let that slide for the moment and come back to it later if I could. "The kids must have come back to you after he died, though. Especially with his second wife going to prison."

Gwen pushed at a strand of gray hair with a capable-looking hand. "They were almost college age by then. In fact, Gregory had left that fall and Diane left the year after. But they were very messed-up kids. Laurence was a strict disciplinarian. Not that I have any quarrel with that—I think kids need structure—but he was a very controlling person, really out of touch with anything emotional, rather aggressive in his manner of dealing with anyone, the kids in particular. So the two of them, after five years of that regime, were both withdrawn and shut-down. Defensive, uncommunicative. From what I could tell, his relation to them was based on attack, being held accountable, much like what he had done with me. Of course, I'd been seeing them alternate weekends and that sort of thing, and I had the usual summer visitation. I just didn't have any idea how far it had gone. And his death was a kick in the head to them on top of that. I'm sure they both had a lot of feelings that were never resolved. Diane went straight into therapy. And Gregory's seen someone since, though not regularly." She paused a moment. "I feel like I'm giving you case histories here."

"Oh no, I appreciate your candor," I said. "Are the kids here in town too?"

"Greg's living south of Palm Springs. Salton Sea. He has a boat down there."

"What sort of work does he do?"

"Well, he doesn't have to do anything. Laurence did provide for them financially. I don't know if you've checked on the insurance yet, but his estate was divided equally between the three kids—Greg, Diane, and Nikki's son, Colin."

"What about Diane? Where is she?"

"She's in Claremont, going to school. Working on another degree. She's interested in teaching deaf children and she seems to do very well. It worried me some at first because I suspect, in her mind, it was all tied up—my divorce, Nikki, Colin, and her responsibility—even though it had nothing to do with her."

"Wait a minute. I don't understand what you mean," I said.

Gwen glanced up at me with surprise. "I thought you'd already talked to Nikki."

"Well, I talked to her once," I said.

"Didn't she tell you Colin was deaf? He was deaf from birth. I don't really remember what caused it, but there was nothing they could do about it apparently. Diane was very upset. She was thirteen, I think, when the baby was born and maybe she resented the intrusion. I don't mean to be so analytical at every turn but some of this came out with her psychiatrist and it seems pertinent. I think now she can articulate most of it herself—in fact she does—so I don't think I'm violating any confidence."

She selected a couple of strands of ribbon from about twenty spools hung on pegboard on the wall above the grooming table. She laid a blue and an orange on Wuffles's head. "What do you think, Wuf? Blue or orange?"

Wuffles raised her (I assumed) eyes and panted happily, and Gwen chose the orange, which I must admit made a certain jaunty sense against Wuffles's silver-gray mop of hair. The dog was docile, full of trust, loving every move even though half of Gwen's attentions turned to me.

"Gregory was into drugs for a while," Gwen said conversationally. "That's what his generation seemed to do while mine was playing house. But he's a good kid and I think he's okay now. Or as okay as he'll ever be. He's happy, which is a lot more than most of us can say—I mean, *I'm* happy but I know a lot of people who aren't."

"Won't he get tired of boating?"

"I hope so," Gwen said lightly. "He can afford to do anything he wants, so if the leisure begins to pall, he'll find something useful to do. He's very smart and he's a very capable kid, in spite of the fact that he's idle right now. Sometimes I envy him that."

"Do you think it would distress the kids if I talked to them?"

Gwen was startled at that, the first time she'd seemed disconcerted by anything. "About their father?"

"I may have to at some point," I said. "I wouldn't like to do it without your knowledge, but it might really help."

"I suppose it would be all right," she said, but her tone was full of misgivings.

"We can talk about it later. It may not be necessary at all."

"Oh. Well. I don't see how it could hurt. I must say, I don't really understand why you're into this business again."

"To see if justice was done, I guess," I said. "It sounds melodramatic, but that's what it amounts to."

"Justice to whom, Laurence or Nikki?"

"Maybe you should tell me what you think. I'm assuming there was no love lost between you and them, but do you think he got his 'just desserts'?"

"Sure, why not? I don't know about her. I figure she had a fair trial and if that's the way it came out, well she must have done it. But there were times I'd have done it myself if I had thought of some way."

"So if she killed him, you wouldn't blame her?"

"Me and half a dozen others. Laurence alienated a lot of people," she said carelessly. "We could have formed a club and sent out a monthly newsletter. I still run into people who sidle up to me and say 'Thank god he's dead.' Literally. Out of the corner of their mouths." Gwen laughed again. "I'm sorry if that sounds irreverent but he was not a nice man."

"But who in particular?"

She put her hand on her hip and gave me a jaded look. "If you got an hour, I'll give you a list," she said.

I laughed then. Her humor seemed irrepressible or maybe she was only feeling ill at ease. Talking to a private eye is often unnerving to people.

Gwen put Wuffles in an empty cage and then went into the other room and led out a big English sheepdog. She lifted its front feet first, placing them on the table, and then she heaved its hind legs up while the dog whined uneasily.

"Oh come on, Duke," she snapped. "This one is such a sissy."

"Do you think we could talk again soon?" I asked.

"Sure, I'd like that. I close up here at six. If you're free then, we can have a drink. By the end of the day, I'm ready for one."

"Me too. I'll see you then," I said.

I hopped down off my stool and let myself out. When the door closed, she was already chatting with the dog. I wondered what else she knew and how much of it she was willing to share. I also hoped to hell I could look that good in another ten years.

THE PATH AT CASA DORINDA

Do not be afraid that our solitude
will be invaded when the path is laid down
through the oak grove we have come to think our own.
the woodpecker taunts with his rat-a-tat-tat
the hawk's head turns full circle
searching for prey atop the sycamore tree
and the hummingbird whirs from his oak branch
to plunder my orange blossoms.
I look beyond the verdant tangle
to the mottled depth of the forest
where Titania sleeps and Puck darts
swift through sun-flecked thickets.

Neighbors on their solitary walks
cannot disturb the primeval splendor
of these groves nor dispel the magic.
They seek solace as we do
knowing that everyone walks the path
leading to the deepest part of the forest
where no sunlight filters through
and cold penetrates and numbs.
What comfort the memory of this dappled sunlight
and the glorious greenness of the green.

Julia Bates
— 1989

CLAIRE RABE

Claire Rabe (b. 1936) has had many writers, including Henry Miller and Kenneth Rexroth, admire her work. Sicily Enough *(1963), originally published by Olympia Press, has since gone through several editions from Capra Press. Lately she has been sharing her impressions with readers of Santa Barbara's* The Independent.

IMPRESSIONS

IT'S NOT WINTER ON THE MESA but the trees are bare. The once abundant, overflowing green of eucalyptus trees has been severely pruned. What was a street by Cezanne has been transformed to Van Gogh. Only at the very top of these tall, fifty-year-old trees, are there thin limbs with a few leaves. Now they cannot drop their heavy branches on houses that stayed small while the trees got big. The mottled, flesh-colored trunks are standing bare but tree cutting has occurred by masters, they've been saved. Next spring they'll prove it. The delight of walking past a row of old trees alive and well inside their hearts! Touching the naked trees is an experience of sculpture, columns of history.

* * *

The night was warm, they sat in their shirt-sleeves on the steps of the office building. Montecito Street was as calm as a lake. The stillness of an industrial neighborhood in the middle of the night. Headlines, deadlines. The absence of traffic was palpable. They spoke softly, enjoying the peace of sitting around on the stoop, drinking coffee, looking at an empty street together, the body of the street no longer covered by the noise and stink of trucks and cars. Intervals of silence. Black verticals of street trees, a

165

feeling of design found in black-and-white films. The darkness and clarity of *Citizen Kane*. The death of Orson Welles.

* * *

Not only surfers ride the dawn of a wild winter storm coming from Point Conception. The furious dialogue between wind and sea, the loud conflict between two forces. Nothing else existed when she was small and heard them in the other room. Decibels of rage. Bartok and Heavy Metal played at the same time. Walking in the rain, that magic action, getting wet, tasting the opal water like a fountain of youth. Avoiding tall trees, observing the lurching crowns of brittle eucalypti. The air so fresh and cool, so breathable. The mud on the road a pleasant substance, something for bare feet.

* * *

Finding the place had been easy, she'd smelled it for years on the freeway near the Milpas exit. The stink dominated the street where her all-important car mechanic was. Salsipuedes—exit if you can!

A fit young chemist was explaining the harmless nature of the pesthole he was working to a committee of homeless and their attorneys inspecting the future site of the Rescue Mission.

The only color in the room was her blue shirt and the glossy brochures showing the logical and pure procession of Santa Barbara's waste into and out of the sewage treatment plant. The room was very well air-conditioned. The enthusiastic chemist, his springy look, did not convince a rugged streetguy wearing shorts with a wool cap on this head: "What about the toxic emissions from here? Would you want your grandmother to live next door?"

The chemist's smile broke the hostile air of the room even though he didn't answer the question. He was just doing his job, showing a healthy person, free of anxiety, but not necessarily free of contaminants.

* * *

166

Gridlock on 101 south and Carrillo, Multi-lanes of freeway have come to a halt under a smog alert and 95 degree heat. The KTMS traffic report is accurate; she's a witness. Her air conditioner is laboring. Other drivers turn their motors off. Windows are rolled down. Getting to know your neighbors on the freeway. Nobody smiles. Burning and choking sensations. Gridlock, smog and heat; this is the entrance to hell, the one Dante never thought of. Fury plus the need for patience stiffen her body into a yogic pose that could turn into rigor mortis . . . at last, movement up ahead. Start the motor, get going, roll up the windows, start the air conditioner, insert the Talking Heads, forget about the faces left and right, regain control of the ivory tower on wheels.

* * *

The tide was sloshing against the steps. There was no beach. A woman stood watching a small child playing at the surf's edge, the waves breaking close, solid. Surely the child was too slight to resist. The undertow in this kind of tide swell was notorious. Was that woman a stranger or a seasoned swimmer who simply did not fear the ocean? Was something foolhardy happening? She wanted to yell at the woman to be careful but then she thought what if she was just injecting her own fear into a perfectly calm situation? As she turned the bend of the stairs going back up she paused and thought maybe she should have.

* * *

A day in late autumn with minus tide all afternoon and many sunsets if you count the colors of the sky. Green and turquoise and then those versions of red that begin with yellow and end in black, when the heat is gone and the personal self becomes silhouette.

* * *

Empty storefronts define the sinister aspect of lower State Street at night with Santa Anas blowing paranoia. Where are the people? The desolate street unreels suspicion. The visual dissolves into a prison where she is trapped in a corridor of silence. A shining black and white cop car cruises into the scene to hold her hand as she crosses the street to her own tank that she wheels outta that movie fast.

* * *

She sat in her car to keep warm. The gas man was late. The new house looked remote and unnecessary. Why was she moving to these icy hills! La Cumbre Peak was blue against the oncoming dark. Sailing the wind was a red-tailed hawk.

* * *

The kiss of winter was brief. She wanted more. A few days of great rain and wind and cold. The mountains expanded with snow. Now Camino Cielo was bare again. The untimely warm air holding so still that the jaundiced face of the Channel Islands floats in smog.

* * *

Emerging from the fog, seeing the pine trees grow arms to Santa Cruz Island as if one could hold it all. Cormorants flying east, the sun electrifies time. Closing her eyes, the distance is clear but not so much that the content is known. What rises in her like a snake of song? What undulates her brain, the ultimate sexual organ?

* * *

Crossing Hammond's Meadow, where the blackberries used to be— enough to eat as many as you wanted —fields thriving under benign ne- glect; meadows are metaphors, green with personal history.

The path to the beach is now a concrete road with lamp posts and driveways ready for cars and condos. Do the monarchs on that eucalyptus know their days together are numbered? Not because the tree is sick, but because the developers are pruning this small sacred body of land between the Biltmore and the Miramar, surfers above and Chumash below.

* * *

At the intersection of Las Positas and State with four directional signals, arrows blinking red and green like sliced watermelons. Her grandbaby smiles and gurgles inside her state of the art car seat. Life is good. Should she drive north or south, is the shopping center on the left better than the one of the right? Ambivalence is delightfully brief, she's in the downstream of traffic, her direction determined by the changing lights.

* * *

The crossing to Santa Cruz Island began with two people intending friendship. Both players were unhappy with the eros of their individual lives. She wanted nothing from him—only to listen to a man tell the story of his life. It was her idea of living, neither reading a book nor writing it.

She was on a forty-foot cutter, with a forty-foot mast. The channel was rough. She expected to be cold and wet, she wanted hardship, but she had not expected nausea. After a few hours she was so ill she asked him to turn back. What mattered most was to end the trip with her girlfriend's lover. Nausea is a saving grace.

IN MONTECITO

In a fashionable suburb of Santa Barbara,
Montecito, there visited me one night at midnight
A scream with breasts. As it hung there in the sweet air
That was always the right temperature, the contractors
Who had undertaken to dismantle it, stripped off
The lips, let the air out of the breasts.
                                          People disappear
Even in Montecito, Greenie Taliaferro,
In her white maillot, her good figure almost firm,
Her old pepper-and-salt hair stripped by the hairdresser
To nothing and dyed platinum—Greenie has left her Bentley.
They have thrown away her electric toothbrush, someone else slips
The key into the lock of her safety-deposit box
At the Crocker-Anglo Bank; her seat at the cricket matches
Is warmed by buttocks less delectable than hers.
Greenie's girdle is empty.
                        A scream hangs there in the night:
They strip off the lips, let the air out of the breasts,
And Greenie has gone into the Greater Montecito
That surrounds Montecito like the echo of a scream.

                                          Randall Jarrell
                                          — 1960

PICO IYER

Pico Iyer (b. 1957) has spent his entire life coming to and going from Santa Barbara, where both his parents have had long teaching careers at UCSB. In recent years he has become well-known for his fine writing, including Falling off the Map *(1993) and* The Lady and the Monk *(1991).*

MY SANTA BARBARA

SANTA BARBARA, FOR ME, is the perfect getaway from the world. Hide-out, sanctuary, secular retreat—call it what you will, it is a way of secreting oneself along the sunlit margins of the world, not in the neon glare, but not exactly out of it. Santa Barbara is a way to disappear into the foothills, or the sea-mist, or the house behind the gates; in many ways, the whole city feels like a collection of privacies, of fiercely guarded silences.

If you want to find stimulation, I tell my friends from elsewhere, stay elsewhere; if you crave excitement, or discipline, or the thick steel girders of close-knit society around you, stay in Pittsburgh. What Santa Barbara has to offer has to do with inwardness, and peace; with giving you the room to think, and the time to follow that thought to fruition.

It is, for me, a kind of Walden-by-the-sea; reserved and sociable, alight with nonintrusive friendliness. Santa Barbara rarely encroaches on me, yet I always feel encircled by it. Santa Barbara, in that sense, is the epitome of what California used to be: a way to live without external pressures, in a vacuum of one's choosing. And like the best Californian places, it is, I suspect, best of all for those who come from outside California.

There is, I have found, a kind of invisible circuit that links the enchanted places of the world, and a certain kind of like-minded soul that travels from one point to the next. And so I have found that whenever I am in some charmed Elysium—Kyoto, say, or the Berkeley Hills, or the Ionian Islands—I seem to meet people from Santa Barbara. Everyone here has probably had the experience of bumping into Santa Barbarans elsewhere, a reflection of the fact that Santa Barbarans travel, and that travelers come to Santa Barbara. And for that reason too, no doubt, Santa Barbara has taken in just enough of the world to be diverse, yet not so much as to lose its sense of self. The only reason to leave Santa Barbara, in fact, is to come back newly appreciative of its charms.

When my house in the hills burned down two years ago (1990), and I was forced to move downtown, suddenly I found a new Santa Barbara, and sometimes, on late November afternoons, going on long walks through the Upper East Side, or along Hendry's Beach, or even down good old State Street, I have to shake myself: If this were Italy, I think, or Greece, or the Cote d'Azur, I would think I had found a kind of paradise. The only reason I am slow to call it paradise is because I call it home.

Most of all, though, I like Santa Barbara because it is so fluid a kind of place, open to new definitions, neither one thing nor the other. By this I mean not just that it has different sides, or that Montecito Street contradicts Montecito, or that the west side of Micheltorena refutes the east. Rather, I mean that it is poised between extremities. It is, for one thing, a human-sized place, too big to be a hall of mirrors, yet too small to be a canyon of glass towers. It is less hard than L.A., yet less soft than Santa Cruz; not culturally sterile, yet not over-heated with competition; not quite Southern California, and not quite Northern. Not all dry nor all wet, it is neither simple workplace nor pure playground. Santa Barbara is an amphibian kind of town, with just enough reality to keep the daydreams going.

Divisions, in fact, tend to blur in the languid, jasmine-scented air. In New York, where you move back and forth between a 47-story corporate tower and a 47-square-foot apartment, you always know where one self ends and the next begins; in Santa Barbara, everything glows together. When I lived in New York, moreover, I used to pine daily for Butterfly

Beach, or the quiet elegance of Kanda Thai restaurant, or the high clear purity of the Vedanta Temple; for all the suspensions of reality that help give one a sense of possibility. Now that I am back in Santa Barbara, I never, ever, look back at New York.

This is, of course, a delicate kind of balance to maintain, and it is easy to feel that our city is beginning to disappear inside the gaping black maw of Greater Los Angeles. For decades Santa Barbara has been just manageable enough and curvy enough, and at just the right distance from hard realities, to serve many fugitive Angelenos as an ideal weekend mistress.

Now, though, with the freeway expanding, and the malls encroaching, and with commuters filling the roads, our ruthless neighbor is threatening to make us legal. I still find solace, though: Santa Barbara has always been in large part a place of people passing through—the student on the campus, the hoboes on the railroads; the tourists at the Mission, the cars lined up at the freeway stoplights. Now, with the 101 lights gone, it may seem more than ever just a place to pass by, at the edge of the world's vision; a city without a center people take to be a place without a heart. And if ever the crowds do stop to take a second look, there are always more hide-outs in the hills.

SANTA BARBARA

So he looked at the ranch on the slopes below
Where the peach-bloom shown like a rosier snow
And the Angelus called like a ghost again
For the purple canyons grew dark and deep;
And the sea and the palm-trees whispered sleep;
But, softly aglow, on her cypressed hill,
Santa Barbara, hushed and still,
Shone like a pearl of that rosary strung
By the brothers in gray when the West was young.

Alfred Noyes
– 1942

BIBLIOGRAPHY

Atherton, Gertrude. *Adventures of a Novelist*. New York: Liveright, 1932.

Bates, Julia. *One Road Down from the Wilderness*. Santa Barbara, California: Fithian Press, 1989.

Blackburn, Thomas C., ed. *December's Child: A Book of Chumash Oral Narratives Collected by John Peabody Harrington*. Berkeley, California: University of California Press, 1975.

Bond, Marshall, Jr. *Adventures with Peons, Princes and Tycoons*. Santa Barbara, California: Star Rover Press, 1983.

Bowers, Edgar. *For Louis Pasteur*. Princeton, New Jersey: Princeton University Press, 1989.

Browne, Francis Fisher. *Volunteer Grain*. 1897.

Buckley, Christopher. *Cruising State Street: Growing Up in Southern California*. Reno, Nevada: University of Nevada Press, 1994.

Bryant, Edwin. *What I Saw in California*. New York: D. Appleton and Company, 1848.

Chase, J. Smeaton. *California Coast Trails*. Boston: Houghton Mifflin Company, 1913.

Collins, Michael. *Castrato*. New York: Donald I. Fine, Inc., 1989.

Dahl, David. *Panic Hour*. Santa Barbara, California: Tsunami Press, 1984.

Dana, Richard Henry. *Two Years Before the Mast*. New York: Harper and Brothers, 1840.

Easton, Robert. *Black Tide*. New York: Delacorte Press, 1972.

Grafton, Sue. *"A" is for Alibi*. New York: Holt, Rinehart & Winston, 1982.

Hazard, Carolyn. *Songs in the Sun*, Boston: Houghton Mifflin Company, 1927.

Hyde, Robert. *Six More at Sixty*. Garden City, New York: Doubleday & Company, 1960.

Iyer, Pico. "My Santa Barbara." *Santa Barbara Magazine*. March/April, 1992.

Jarrell, Randall. *The Woman at the Washington Zoo*. New York: Farrar, Strauss & Giroux, 1960.

Laird, Carobeth. *Encounter With an Angry God: Recollections of My Life with John Peabody Harrington*. Banning, California: Malki Museum Press, 1975.

Loomis, Edward. Unpublished poem.

Macdonald, Ross. *The Underground Man*. New York: Alfred A. Knopf, Inc., 1971.

Millar, Margaret. *The Birds and the Beasts Were There*. New York: Random House, 1967.

Noyes, Alfred. *Poems of the New World*. Philadelphia: J.B. Lippincott Co., 1942.

Portugés, Paul. *Paper Song*. Santa Barbara, California: Ross-Erikson, Publishers, 1984.

Rabe, Claire. *Sicily Enough and More*. Santa Barbara, California: Capra Press, 1989.

Robinson, Alfred. *Life in California*. Salt Lake City: Peregrine Publishers, 1970.

Sanborn, Kate. *A Truthful Woman in Southern California*. New York: D. Appleton and Company, 1893.

Spaulding, Edward Selden. *Venison and a Breath of Sage*. Santa Barbara, California: W.T. Genns, 1967.

Stephens. Alan, *Selected Poems*. Chicago: Swallow Press, 1982.

Teasdale, Sara. *Stars To-Night*. New York: The Macmillan Commpany, 1930.

Turner, Frederick. *Between Two Lives*. Middletown, Connecticut: Wesleyan University Press, 1970.

Von K., Camilla K. *Sea-Leaves*. Santa Barbara, California, 1884.

White, Stewart Edward. *The Mountains*. New York: McClure, Phillips & Company, 1904.

NOTES ON POETS

Camilla K. von K. was the pseudonym of Mary C.F. Hall Wood, whose collection of poems, *Sea-Leaves,* was one of the earliest books to come out of Santa Barbara. Francis Fisher Browne (1843-1913) was the founding editor of *Dial,* the leading literary magazine of its day, which he edited from Santa Barbara during the years before his death.

Sara Teasdale (1884-1933) was a popular poet in the early years of the century. She spent a half year in Santa Barbara in 1919, writing a number of poems inspired by the town. Caroline Hazard (1856-1945) was a poet, biographer and president of Wellesley College. Her family had a long connection with Santa Barbara. Their home, known as "Mission Hill," next to the Mission, is now St. Mary's Retreat.

The English poet Alfred Noyes (1880-1958) lived in Santa Barbara in the World War II years. Randall Jarrell (1914-65) is generally considered one of the finest post-World War II American poets.

Edgar Bowers (b. 1924), Edward Loomis (b. 1924) and Alan Stephens (b. 1925) have published widely and have taught in the English Department at the University of California at Santa Barbara (UCSB) for many years.

Frederick Turner (b. 1943) taught briefly at UCSB in the 1970s and is a poet, critic and literary historian. David Dahl, poet and printer, attended UCSB. Paul Portugés is a screenwriter and farmer, as well as a poet, who makes his home in Santa Barbara.

Julia Bates (b. 1909) has written sensitively of her life in California as well as her earlier New England days.

PERMISSIONS

The excerpts reprinted in this book have been reprinted by permission as follows:

December's Child ed. Thomas C. Blackburn. Reprinted by permission of University of California Press.

Edgar Bowers, "The Courthouse," from *For Louis Pasteur.* Copyright 1989 by Edgar Bowers. Reprinted by permission of Princeton University Press.

Cruising State Street by Christopher Buckley first appeared in *Santa Barbara Magazine,* November/December 1991. Reprinted by permission of Christopher Buckley.

Michael Collins, "The Car that Cuts You Off," from *Castrato.* Copyright 1989 by Dennis Lynds. Reprinted by permission of Donald I. Fine, Inc.

Black Tide by Robert Easton. Reprinted by permission of Robert Easton.

Sue Grafton, "The Groomer," from *"A" is for Alibi.* Copyright 1982 by Sue Grafton. Reprinted by permission of Henry Holt & Co., Inc.

Robert Hyde, "Six More at Sixty," from *Six More at Sixty.* Copyright 1960 by Robert Hyde. Reprinted by permission of the estate of Florence Tuckerman Hyde.

"My Santa Barbara" by Pico Iyer first appeared in *Santa Barbara Magazine,* March/April 1992. Reprinted by permission of Pico Iyer.

Randall Jarrell, "In Montecito," from *The Complete Poems* by Randall Jarrell. Copyright 1969 by Mrs. Randall Jarrell. Reprinted by permission of Farrar, Straus & Giroux, Inc.

Encounter with an Angry God by Carobeth Laird. Reprinted by permission of Malki Museum Press.

Ross Macdonald, "The Underground Man," from *The Underground Man.* Copyright 1971 by Ross Macdonald. Reprinted by permission of Alfred A. Knopf, Inc.

Margaret Millar, "The Coyote Fire," from *The Birds and the Beasts Were There.* Copyright 1967 by Margaret Millar. Reprinted by permission of the Margaret Millar Suvivor's Trust u/a 4/12/82.

"Impressions" by Claire Rabe. Reprinted by permission of Claire Rabe.

Venison and a Breath of Sage by Edward Selden Spaulding. Reprinted by permission of Edward R. Spaulding.

Frederick Turner, "Santa Barbara, 1970," from *Between Two Lives.* Copyright 1972 Wesleyan University Press. Reprinted by permission of the University Press of New England.